Streamers

by David Rabe

A SAMUEL FRENCH ACTING EDITION

FOUNDED 1830

NEW YORK HOLLYWOOD LONDON TORONTO

SAMUELFRENCH.COM

ISBN 978-0-573-64019-3   Printed in U.S.A.   #1005

IMPORTANT BILLING AND CREDIT REQUIREMENTS

All producers of *STREAMERS* *must* give credit to the Author of the Play in all programs distributed in connection with performances of the Play, and in all instances in which the title of the Play appears for the purposes of advertising, publicizing or otherwise exploiting the Play and/or a production. The name of the Author *must* appear on a separate line on which no other name appears, immediately following the title and *must* appear in size of type not less than fifty percent of the size of the title type.

STREAMERS was produced by the Long Wharf Theater on January 30, 1976 under the direction of Mike Nichols. The set design was by Tony Walton, the costumes were by Bill Walker, lighting was by Ronald Wallace. The production was stage managed by Nina Seely. The cast was as follows:

RICHIE . . . . Peter Evans

MARTIN. . . . . Michael-Raymond O'Keefe

CARLYLE. . . . . .Joe Fields

BILLY. . . . . .John Heard

ROGER . . . . .Herbert Jefferson Jr.

SGT. ROONEY. . . . . Kenneth McMillan

SGT. COKES . . . . Dolph Sweet

M.P. LIEUTENANT . . . . .Stephen Mendillo

PFC HINSON. . . . . .Ron Siebert

PFC CLARK . . . . Michael Kell

STREAMERS was produced in New York by Joseph Papp (Bernard Gersten, Associate Producer) on April 21, 1976 at the Mitzi Newhouse Theater at Lincoln Center under the direction of Mike Nichols. The set design was by Tony Walton, the costumes were by Bill Walker, lighting was by Ronald Wallace. The production was stage managed by Nina Seely. The cast was as follows:

RICHIE . . . . Peter Evans

MARTIN. . . . . Michael Kell

CARLYLE. . . . . .Dorian Harewood

BILLY. . . . . Paul Rudd

ROGER . . . . Terry Alexander

SGT. ROONEY. . . . . Kenneth McMillan

SGT. COKES . . . . Dolph Sweet

M.P. LIEUTENANT . . . . .Arlen Dean Snyder

PFC HINSON. . . . . Les Roberts

PFC CLARK . . . . .Mark Metcalf

PFC . . . . .Miklos Horvath

STREAMERS was presented by Roundabout Theatre Company (Todd Haimes, Artistic Director) in New York City on November 11, 2008. It was directed by Scott Ellis, set design was by Neil Patel, lighting design was by Jeff Croiter, costume design was by Tom Broecker, sound design and original music was by John Gromada, and fight direction was by Rick Sordelet. The production stage manager was Stephen M. Kaus. The cast was as follows:

RICHIE	Hale Appleman
MARTIN	Charlie Hewson
CARLYLE	Ato Essandoh
BILLY	Brad Fleischer
ROGER	JD Williams
SGT. ROONEY	John Sharian
SGT. COKES	Larry Clarke
M.P. LIEUTENANT	Cobey Mandarino
PFC HINSON	E.J. Cantu
PFC CLARK	Jason McDowell-Green
PFC	Alex Avin, Jr.

CHARACTERS

RICHIE

MARTIN

CARLYLE

BILLY

ROGER

SGT. ROONEY

SGT. COKES

M.P. LIEUTENANT

PFC HINSON

PFC CLARK

PFC

A NOTE ON THE TEXT

The revisions in this text were done in cooperation with the Roundabout production in November of 2008. Though a few of the revisions had another rationale, the primary purpose was to set the play emphatically in its time period of late 1965.

ACT ONE

*(The set is a large cadre room thrusting angularly toward the audience. The floor is wooden and brown. Brightly waxed in places, it is worn and dull in other sections. The back wall is brown and angled, putting the room slightly off kilter. Along the back wall there are three windows that open on a passageway formed by the wall of another building. Against the back wall of the cadre room stand three wall lockers. **RICHIE**'s is the furthest stage right and **BILLY**'s is next to it. They are side by side and stage right of the middle window. The third locker, **ROGER**'s, is to the stage left side of the window. A chair stands against the wall in front of the middle window. Stage right is the door that runs to a hall with a screen door to the outside and down the hall are latrines, showers, other cadre rooms, and larger barracks. There are three bunks. **BILLY**'s bunk is parallel to **ROGER**'s bunk. The foot of both of these bunks are downstage. **RICHIE**'s bunk is at a right angle to the wall and the other bunks, jutting out from the stage right wall. At the foot of each bunk is a green wooden footlocker. There is an electrical outlet that **ROGER** uses for his radio. A reading lamp is clamped onto the metal piping at the head of each bunk. A wooden chair stands beside the wall lockers upstage, another near the door, and a third in the stage left corner. Two mops hang off the wall near the door and a trash can.)*

*(It is dusk. 1965. As the lights rise on the room, **RICHIE** is seated and bowed forward on his bunk. He wears his long-sleeved khaki summer dress uniform. **MARTIN**, a thin young man, paces, worried. A white bandage stained red with blood is wrapped around his wrist. He paces several steps and falters, stops. He stands there.)*

9

RICHIE. *(hushed, gentle)* Honest to God, Martin, I don't know what to say anymore. I don't know what to tell you.

MARTIN. *(beginning to pace again)* I mean it. I just can't stand it. Look at me.

RICHIE. *(trying to help)* I know.

MARTIN. I hate it.

RICHIE. We've got to make up a story. They'll ask you a hundred questions.

MARTIN. Do you know I hate it?

RICHIE. Everybody does. Don't you think I hate it, too?

MARTIN. I enlisted though. I enlisted and I hate it.

RICHIE. I enlisted, too.

MARTIN. I vomit every morning. I get the dry heaves. In the middle of every night.

(He flops down on the corner of **BILLY**'s *bunk and sits there slumped forward, shaking his head.)*

RICHIE. You can stop that. You can.

MARTIN. No.

RICHIE. You're just scared. It's just fear.

MARTIN. They're all so mean; they're all so awful. I've got two years to go. Just thinking about it is going to make me sick. I thought it would be different from the way it is.

RICHIE. But you could have died, for God's sake.

MARTIN. I just wanted out.

RICHIE. I might not have found you, though. I might not have gone in there.

(as pop music is heard in the hall)

MARTIN. I don't care. I'd be out.

(The door opens and a black man in civilian clothes, circa 1965 steps in. He has a large transistor radio stacked on his shoulder, right up to his ear, and Baby Love, by the Supremes is playing loudly. This is **CAR-LYLE.** *He bops to the music, looking around as* **RICHIE** *moves toward him.)*

RICHIE. No. Roger isn't here right now.

CARLYLE. Who isn't?

RICHIE. He isn't here.

CARLYLE. They told me a black boy livin' in here. *(looking suspiciously about the room)* I don't see him.

RICHIE. That's what I'm saying. He isn't here. He'll be back later. You can come back later. His name is Roger.

*(**MARTIN** thrusts the bloody, bandaged wrist toward **CARLYLE**.)*

MARTIN. I slit my wrist.

RICHIE. Martin! Jesus!

MARTIN. I did.

RICHIE. He's kidding. He's kidding.

CARLYLE. What was his name? Martin? *(He is confused, and confusion makes him angry.)* You are Martin?

MARTIN. Yes.

*(As **BILLY**, a white in his mid-twenties, blond and trim, appears in the door, carrying a slice of pie on a paper napkin. The room is a hubbub with the music, the stranger, **RICHIE** up on his feet, **MARTIN** tense.)*

BILLY. Hey, what's goin' on?

CARLYLE. Nothin' man. Not a thing.

*(**CARLYLE** turns and leaves and **BILLY** looks questioningly at **RICHIE**. He places the piece of pie on the chair beside the door and crosses to his bunk.)*

RICHIE. He came in looking for Roger, but he didn't even know his name.

BILLY. *(Sitting on his bunk, he starts taking off his shoes.)* How come you weren't at dinner, Rich? I brought you a piece of pie. Hey, Martin.

MARTIN. *(thrusting out his towel-wrapped wrist)* I cut my wrist, Billy.

RICHIE. Oh, for God's sake, Martin!

BILLY. Huh?

MARTIN. I did.

RICHIE. You are disgusting, Martin.

MARTIN. No. It's the truth. I did. I am not disgusting.

RICHIE. Well, maybe it isn't disgusting, but it certainly is disappointing.

BILLY. What are you guys talking about? *(Sitting there, he really doesn't know what is going on.)*

MARTIN. I cut my wrists. I slashed them, and Richie is pretending I didn't.

RICHIE. *(These distinctions are of great importance.)* I am not. And you only cut one wrist, and you didn't slash it.

MARTIN. I can't stand the army anymore, Billy. *(moving to petition **BILLY**)*

RICHIE. *(stepping between **MARTIN** and **BILLY**)* Billy, listen to me. This is between Martin and me.

MARTIN. It's between me and the army, Richie.

RICHIE. *(taking **MARTIN** by the shoulders)* Let's just go outside and talk, Martin. You don't know what you're saying.

BILLY. Can I see? I mean, did he really do it? *(trying to get a better look at **MARTIN**'s wrist)*

RICHIE. No!

MARTIN. I did.

BILLY. That's awful. Jesus. Maybe you should go to the infirmary.

RICHIE. I washed it with peroxide. It's not deep. Just let us be. Please. He needs to straighten out his thinking a little, that's all.

BILLY. Well, maybe I could help him.

MARTIN. Maybe he could.

RICHIE. *(exasperated, pushing **MARTIN** to get him out the door)* Get out of here, Martin. Billy, you do some push-ups or something.

BILLY. No.

RICHIE. I know what Martin needs.

*(He whirls and rushes into the hall after **MARTIN**, leaving **BILLY** scrambling to get his shoes on.)*

BILLY. You're no doctor, are you? I just want to make sure he doesn't have to go to the infirmary, then I'll leave you alone.

(With one shoe on, he grabs up the second and runs out the door into the hall after them.)

Martin! Martin, wait up!

(Silence. The door has been left open. Fifteen or twenty seconds pass. Then someone is heard coming down the hall. He is singing "Get a Job" and trying to do the voices and harmonies of a vocal group. **ROGER**, *a tall, well-built black man in long sleeved khakis, comes in the door. He has a laundry bag over his shoulder, a pair of clean civilian trousers, and a shirt on a hanger in his other hand. After dropping the bag on his bunk, he goes to his wall locker, where he carefully hangs up the civilian clothes. Returning to the bunk, he picks up the laundry and then, as if struck, he throws the bag down on the bunk, tears off his tie, and sits down angrily on the bunk. For a moment, with his head in his hands, he sits there. Then, resolutely, he rises, takes up the position of attention, and simply topples forward, his hands leaping out to break his fall at the last instant and putting him into the push-up position. Counting in a hissing, whispering voice, he does ten push-ups before giving up and flopping onto his belly. He simply doesn't have the will to do any more. Lying there, he counts rapidly on.)*

ROGER. Fourteen, fifteen. Twenty. Twenty-five.

*(**BILLY**, shuffling thoughtfully back in, sees **ROGER** lying there. **ROGER** springs to his feet, heads towards his footlocker, out of which he takes an ashtray and a pack of cigarettes.)*

ROGER. You come into this area, you come in here marchin', boy: standin' tall.

*(**BILLY**, having gone to his wall locker, tosses a Playboy magazine onto his bunk, before removing shoe polish and a rag from his footlocker.)*

BILLY. I was marchin'.

ROGER. You call that marchin'?

BILLY. I was as tall as I am; I was marchin' – what do you want?

ROGER. Outa here, man; outa this goddamn typin'-terrors outfit and into some kinda real army. Or else out and free.

BILLY. So what's stoppin' you; get out. Go on.

ROGER. Ain't you a bitch.

BILLY. You and me more regular army than the goddamn sergeants around this place, you know that?

ROGER. I was you, Billy boy, I wouldn't be talking' so sacrilegious so loud, or they be doin' you like they did the ole sarge.

BILLY. He'll get off.

ROGER. Sheee-it, he'll get off.

(Sitting down on the side of his bunk, facing BILLY, ROGER lights up a cigarette, as BILLY begins spit-shining his shoes.)

ROGER. Don't you think L.B.J. want to have some sergeants in that Vietnam, man? In Disneyland, baby? Lord have mercy on the ole sarge. He's goin' over there to be Mickey Mouse.

BILLY. Do him a lot of good. Make a man outa him.

ROGER. That's right, that's right. He said the same damn thing about himself and you, too, I do believe. You know what's the ole boy's MOS? His military Occupation Specialty? Demolitions, baby. Expert is his name.

BILLY. *(barely glancing up from the task)* You're kiddin' me.

ROGER. Do I jive?

BILLY. You mean that poor ole bastard who cannot light his own cigar for shakin' is supposed to go over there blowin' up bridges and shit? Do they wanna win this war or not, man?

ROGER. Ole sarge was over in Europe in the big one, Billy. Did all kinds a bad things.

BILLY. Was he drinkin' since he got the word?

ROGER. Was he breathin', Billy? Was he breathin'?

BILLY. Well at least he ain't cuttin' his fuckin' wrists.

(Silence. **ROGER** *looks at* **BILLY,** *who keeps on working.)*

BILLY. Man, that's the real damn army over there ain't it? That ain't shinin' your shoes and standin' tall. And we might end up in it, man.

*(***ROGER,*** *rising, begins to sort his laundry.)*

BILLY. Roger – You ever ask yourself if you'd rather fight in a war where it was freezin' cold, or one where there was awful snakes? You ever ask that question?

ROGER. Can't say I ever did.

BILLY. We used to ask it all the time. All the time. I mean, us kids sittin' out on the back porch tellin' ghost stories at night. 'Cause it was Korea time, and the newspapers were fulla pictures of soldiers in snow with white frozen beards; they got these rags tied around their feet. And snakes. We hated snakes. Hated 'em. I mean, it's bad enough to be in the jungle duckin' bullets, but then you crawl right into a goddamn snake. That's awful. That's awful.

ROGER. It don't sound none too good.

BILLY. I got my draft notice, goddamn Vietnam didn't even exist.

BILLY. I mean, it existed, but not as in a war we might be in. I started crawlin' around the floor a this house where I was stayin' 'cause I'd dropped outa school, and I was goin' "Bang, bang" pretendin'. Jesus.

ROGER. My first goddamn formation in basic, Billy, this NCO's up there jammin' away about how some a us are goin' to be dyin' in the war. I'm sayin', "what war? What that crazy man talkin' about?"

BILLY. Us, too. I couldn't believe it. I couldn't believe it. And now we got three people goin' from here.

ROGER. Five.

(They look at each other, and then turn away, each returning to his task.)

BILLY. It don't seem possible. I mean, people shootin' at you. Shootin' at you to kill you. *(slight pause)* It's somethin'.

(Putting away the polish, he retrieves a straight razor and whetstone.)

ROGER. What did you decide you preferred?

BILLY. Huh?

*(Back on his bed, **BILLY** sharpens the razor, while, **ROGER**, continuing with his laundry, tries for a joke.)*

ROGER. Did you decide you would prefer the snakes or would you prefer the snow? 'Cause it look like it is going to be the snakes.

BILLY. I think I had pretty much made up my mind on the snow.

ROGER. Well, you just let 'em know that Billy. Maybe they can get one goin' special just for you up in Alaska. You can go to the Klondike. Fightin' some snowmen.

*(**RICHIE** comes into the room and shuts the door.)*

RICHIE. Hi, hi, hi everybody. Billy, hello.

BILLY. Hey.

ROGER. What's happenin', Rich?

(Crossing to his wall locker, he pulls off his tie. Tossing the tie into the locker, he begins unbuttoning the cuffs of his shirt.)

RICHIE. I simply did this rather wonderful thing for a friend of mine, helped him see himself in a clearer, more hopeful light – a little room in his life for hope. And I feel very good. Didn't Billy tell you?

*(Moving to the chair beside the door, **RICHIE** picks up the pie **BILLY** left there.)*

ROGER. About what?

RICHIE. About Martin.

(Placing the pie atop his locker, he sits on his footlocker to remove his shoes and socks.)

ROGER. No.

BILLY. *(looking up and speaking pointedly)* No.

(He moves his locker to put away the razor and whetstone)

RICHIE. No? No?

BILLY. What do I wanna gossip about Martin for?

*(**RICHIE** can't figure out what is going on with **BILLY.** With his shoes and socks in hand, he heads for his wall locker, and **BILLY** avoids him, going back to his bunk.)*

RICHIE. Who was planning to gossip? I mean, it did happen. We could talk about it. I mean, I wasn't hearing his goddamn confession. Oh, my sister told me Catholics were boring.

BILLY. Good thing I ain't one anymore.

RICHIE. *(taking off his shirt)* It really wasn't anything, Roger, except Martin made this rather desperate, pathetic gesture for attention that seems to have brought to the surface Billy's more humane and protective side. *(Reaching out, he tousels **BILLY**'s hair.)*

BILLY. Man, I am gonna have to obliterate you.

RICHIE. *(tossing his shirt into his locker)* I don't know what you're so embarrassed about.

BILLY. I just think Martin's got enough trouble without me yappin' to everybody.

RICHIE. *(moving nearer **BILLY,** playful and teasing)* "Obliterate"? "Obliterate" did you just say? Oh, Billy, you better say "shit" "ain't" and "motherfucker" real quick now, or we'll all know just how far beyond the fourth grade you went.

ROGER. *(having moved to his locker, into which he is placing his folded clothes)* You hear about the ole sarge, Richard?

BILLY. *(grinning)* You ain't – shit – motherfucker.

ROGER. *(laughing)* All right.

(As **BILLY** *reaches out to* **ROGER** *and they slap hands,* **RICHIE** *watches)*

RICHIE. *(very droll)* Billy, no, no. Wit is my domain. You're in charge of sweat and running around the block.

ROGER. You wanna hear about the ole sarge?

RICHIE. What about the ole sarge? Oh, who cares. Let's go to a movie. Billy, wanna? Let's go, C'mon.

(He hurries to his locker, beginning to remove his trousers.)

BILLY. Sure. What's playin'?

RICHIE. I don't know. Can't remember. Something good, though.

(With a Playboy magazine from his locker, **ROGER** *is settling down on his bunk, his back toward both* **BILLY** *and* **RICHIE.** *)*

BILLY. You wanna go, Rog?

RICHIE. Don't ask Roger! *(Irritated for a split second, but he covers with a joke quickly.)* How are we going to kiss and hug and stuff if he's there?

BILLY. That ain't funny, man.

*(***BILLY** *is stretched out on his bunk, and* **RICHIE** *strides over to flop down, as if to lie beside him.)*

RICHIE. And what time will you pick me up?

BILLY. *(pushing* **RICHIE** *off the bunk onto the floor)* Well, you just fall down and wait, all right?

RICHIE. *(Leaping to his feet, he heads to his locker to remove his shorts, put on a robe.)* Can I help it if I love you?

ROGER. You gonna take a shower, Richard?

RICHIE. Cleanliness is nakedness, Roger.

ROGER. Is that right? I didn't know that. Not too many people know that. You may be the only person in the world who know that.

RICHIE. And godliness is in there somewhere, of course.

(Putting a towel around his neck, **RICHIE** *gathers toiletries to carry to the shower.)*

ROGER. You got your own way a lookin' at things, man. You cute.

RICHIE. That's right.

ROGER. You g'wan, have a good time in that shower.

RICHIE. Oh, I will.

BILLY. *(without looking up from his task)* And don't drop your soap.

RICHIE. I will if I want to.

(Already out the door, he slams it shut with a flourish.)

BILLY. Can you imagine bein' in combat with Richie – people blastin' away at you, he'd probably want to hold your hand.

ROGER. Ain't he something'?

BILLY. Who's zat?

ROGER. He's all right.

BILLY. *(heading toward his wall locker to put away his Dopp kit)* Sure he is, except he's livin' under water.

*(Looking at **BILLY**, **ROGER** senses something unnerving; it makes **ROGER** rise, and return his magazine to his footlocker.)*

ROGER. I think we oughta do this area, man. I think we oughta do our area. Mop and buff this floor.

BILLY. You really don't think he means that shit he talks, do you?

ROGER. Huh? Awwww, man – Billy, no.

BILLY. I'd put money on it, Roger, and I ain't got much money.

*(**BILLY** is trying to face **ROGER** with this, but **ROGER**, seated on his bunk, has turned away. He is unbuttoning his shirt.)*

ROGER. Man, no, no. I'll tellin' you, lad, you listen to the ole Rog. You seen that picture a that little dolly he's got in his locker? He ain't swish, man, believe me – he's cool.

BILLY. It's just that ever since we been in this room, he's been different somehow. Somethin'.

ROGER. No, he ain't.

BILLY. You ever talk to any a these guys – queers I mean? You ever sit down, just rap with one of 'em?

ROGER. Hell, no; what I wanna do that for? Shit, no.

BILLY. I mean, some of 'em are okay guys, just way up this bad alley, and you say to 'em, "I'm straight, be cool," they go their own way. But then there's these other ones, these bitches, man, and they're so crazy they think anybody can be had. Because they been had themselves. So you tell 'em you're straight, and they just nod and smile. You ain't real to 'em. They can't see nothin' but themselves and these goddamn games they're always playin'. *(Having returned to his bunk, he is putting on his shoes.)* I mean, you can be decent about anything, Roger, you see what I'm sayin'? We're all just people, man, and some of us are hardly that. That's all I'm sayin'. *(There is a slight pause as he sits there thinking. Then he gets to his feet.)* I'll go get some buckets and stuff so we can clean up, okay? This area's a mess. This area ain't standin' tall.

ROGER. That's good talk, lad; this area a midget you put it next to an area standin' tall.

BILLY. Got to be good fuckin' troopers.

ROGER. That's right, that's right. I know the meanin' of the words.

BILLY. I mean, I just think we all got to be honest with each other – you understand me?

ROGER. No, I don't understand you; one stupid fuckin' nigger like me – how's that gonna be?

BILLY. That's right; mock me, man. That's what I need. I'll go get the wax.

(BILLY goes, leaving the door open. ROGER sits, thinking, and then he looks at RICHIE's locker and walks to the locker which he opens. He looks at the Playboy pinup hanging on the inside of the door. Shaking his head in awe, he takes an step backward.)

ROGER. Sheee-it.

*(Through the open door behind **ROGER** comes **CAR-LYLE**. **CARLYLE** is now dressed in filthy, grease-stained fatigues, a messy fatigue jacket. He studies **ROGER**, who is oblivious, still gazing dreamily at the Playboy pinup.)*

CARLYLE. Boy – whose locker you lookin' into?

ROGER. *(whirling, startled, but recovering quickly)* Hey, baby, what's happenin'

CARLYLE. That ain't your locker, is what I'm askin, nigger. I mean, you ain't got no white goddamn woman hangin' or your wall.

ROGER. Oh, no – no, no.

CARLYLE. You don't wanna be lyin' to me, 'cause I got to turn you in you lyin' and you do got the body a some white goddamn woman hangin' there for you to peek at nobody around but you – you can be thinkin' about that sweet wet pussy an' maybe it hot, an' maybe it cool.

ROGER. I could be thinkin' all that, except I know the penalty for lyin'.

CARLYLE. Thank God for that. *(extending his hand, palm up)*

ROGER. That's right. This here the locker of a faggot. *(He slaps **CARLYLE**'s hand, palm to palm.)*

CARLYLE. Course it is; I see that; any damn body know that.

*(**ROGER** crosses toward his bunk and **CARLYLE** swaggers about pulling a pint of whiskey from his hip pocket.)*

CARLYLE. You want a shot? Have you a little taste, my man.

ROGER. Naw.

CARLYLE. C'mon. C'mon. I think you a Tom you don't drink outa my bottle.

*(He thrusts the bottle toward **ROGER** and wipes a sweat- and grease stained sleeve across his mouth.)*

ROGER. *(taking the bottle)* Shit.

CARLYLE. That right. How do I know? I just got in. New boy in town. Somewhere over there; I dunno. They dump me in amongst a whole bunch a pale, boring motherfuckers. *(exploring the room)* I just come in from P Company, man, and I been all over this place, don't see too damn many of us. This outfit look like it a little short on soul. I been walkin' all around, I tell you, and the number is small. Like one hand you can tabulate the lot of 'em. We got few brothers I been able to see is what I'm sayin'. You and me and two cats down in the small bay. That's all I found. What day is it, man?

ROGER. What?

CARLYLE. What day is it? I wanna know what day it is?

ROGER. Saturday.

CARLYLE. *(taking a small tear-away calendar from his pocket)* We in November yet, or still stuck in fucking October?

ROGER. What you got against October, man?

CARLYLE. I got to know how many days I got to go in this fucked up shitty assed army, man. They runnin' me so hard I can't keep my mind right, you know. But I forget to tear it out sometimes. *(flipping the remaining pages)* You sure it ain't November?

ROGER. No, Soul. It's October. Saturday, the 30th 1965.

CARLYLE. Fucked up. *(Tearing out and crumpling a page, he tosses it on the floor.)*

ROGER. I guess.

(As ROGER *is about to hand the bottle back,* CARLYLE *almost angrily waves him off.)*

CARLYLE. No, no, you take another; take you a real taste.

ROGER. It ain't so bad here. We do alright.

CARLYLE. *(moves about warily)* How about the white guys? They give you any sweat? What's the situation? No jive. I like to know what is goin' on with the situation before that situation get a chance to be closin' in on me.

ROGER. *(Setting the bottle on the footlocker, he sits down.)* Man, I'm tellin' you, it ain't bad. They're just pale, most of 'em, you know. They can't help it; how they gonna help it? Some of 'em got little bit a soul, couple real good boys around this way. Get 'em little bit of Coppertone, they be straight, man.

CARLYLE. How about the NCO's? We got any brother NCO watchin' out for us or they all white, like I goddamn well KNOW all the officers are? Fuckin' officers always white, man; fuckin' snow cones and bars everywhere you look. Couple minutes ago, you see what I'm sayin' – this goddamn corporal got to get in my face tellin' me I can't play my radio. He's the man, tellin' me nigger shut it off, get in your fatigues, you ain't on the street. I know I ain't on the street, motherfucker. I hate this damn army. *(He is restless, agitated, moving to his right, his left.)*

ROGER. First sergeant's a black man.

CARLYLE. All right; good news. Hey, you wanna go over the club with me, or maybe downtown? I got wheels. Let's be free. *(rushing at* **ROGER***)* Let's be free.

ROGER. Naw –

CARLYLE. Ohhh, baby – !

(He tugs wildly at **ROGER** *to get him to the door.)*

ROGER. Some other time. *(pulling free)* I gotta get the area straight. Me and the guy sleeps in here too are gonna shape the place up a little.

*(***CARLYLE** *cannot understand. It hurts him, depresses him as he looks the room over.)*

CARLYLE. You got a sweet deal here an' you wanna keep it, that right? How you rate you get a room like this for yourself – you and a couple guys? *(Pacing about, he opens a footlocker, looks inside.)*

ROGER. Spec 4. The three of us here are Spec 4.

CARLYLE. You get a room then, huh? *(Suddenly, furious, bewildered by what he's heard, but knowing he will never have such a room.)* Oh, man, I hate this goddamn army. I hate this bastard army. I mean, I just got outa basic – off leave – you know? Back on the block for two weeks – and now here. They don't pull any a that petty shit, now, do they – that goddamn petty basic training bullshit? They do and I'm gonna be bustin' some head – my hand is gonna be upside all kinds a heads, 'cause I ain't gonna be able to endure it, man, not that kinda

crap – understand? *(And again, he is rushing at* **ROGER**.*)*
Hey, hey, oh, c'mon, let's get my wheels and make it,
man, do me the favor.

ROGER. How'm I gonna? I got my obligations.

*(**CARLYLE** spins away, hurt, angry.)*

CARLYLE. Jesus, baby, can't you remember the outside?
How long it been since you been on leave? It is so
sweet out there, nigger; you got it all forgot. I had such
a sweet, sweet time. They doin' dances Baby, make
you want to cry. Them niggers in Watts got their shit
straight, man – burnin' it down. Burn baby burn. You
know what I mean, Soul?

ROGER. Sure.

CARLYLE. I had a bad scene in basic – up the hill and down
the hill; it ain't something I enjoyed even a little. So
they do me wrong here, Jim, they gonna be sorry.
Some-damn-body. *(At first halfway mocking himself, his
fear becomes real and almost trance-like.)* And this whole
Vietnam THING – I do not dig it. Lord, Lord, don't
let 'em touch me. Christ, what will I do, they DO!
Whooooooooooo!

(Freezing, as he feels **ROGER** *looking at him, he hastily
gets his act together.)*

CARLYLE. And they pullin' guys outa here, too, ain't they?
Pullin' 'em like weeds, man; throwin' 'em into the fire.
It's shit, man.

ROGER. They got this ole sarge sleeps down the hall – just
today they got him.

CARLYLE. Which ole sarge?

ROGER. He sleeps just down the hall. Big guy.

CARLYLE. Wino, right?

ROGER. Boozehound.

CARLYLE. Yeh; I seen him. They got him, huh?

ROGER. He's goin'; gotta be packin' his bags. And three
other guys two days ago. And two guys last week.

CARLYLE. Ohhh, them bastards. And everybody just takes it. It ain't our war, brother. I'm tellin' you. That's what gets me, nigger. It ain't our war nohow, because it ain't our country, and that's what burns my ass – that and everybody just sittin' and takin' it. They gonna be bustin' balls, man – kickin' and stompin'. Everybody here maybe one week from shippin' out to get blown clean away and, man, whata they doin? They doin' what they told. That what they doin'. Like you? Shit! You gonna straighten up your goddamn area! Well, that ain't for me; I'm gettin' hat, and makin' it out where it's sweet and the people's livin'. I can't cut this jive here, man. I'm tellin' you. I can't cut it.

(He has ended up close to **ROGER** *who is near his bunk. Behind him now.* **RICHIE** *enters, his hair wet, traces of shaving cream on his face. Toweling his hair, he falters, seeing* **CARLYLE.** *Then he crosses to his locker.* **CARLYLE** *grins at* **ROGER,** *steps toward* **RICHIE** *and gives a little bow.)*

CARLYLE. My name is Carlyle, what is yours?

RICHIE. Richie.

CARLYLE. *(glancing to* **ROGER** *to share his joke)* Hello. Where is Martin? That cute little Martin.

*(***RICHIE** *has just taken off his robe, and with his back turned is hastily pulling on his underwear as* **CARLYLE** *turns back and sees him.)*

CARLYLE. You cute too, Richie.

RICHIE. Martin doesn't live here.

CARLYLE. *(Watching* **RICHIE,** *he slowly turns toward* **ROGER.)** You ain't gonna make it with me, man?

ROGER. Naw – like I tole you. I'll catch you later.

CARLYLE. That's sad, man; make me cry in my heart.

ROGER You g'wan get your head smokin'. Stop on back.

CARLYLE. Okay, okay. Got to be one man one more time. *(on the move for the door, his hand extended palm up behind him, demanding the appropriate response)* Baby! Gimme! Gimme!

(Lunging, **ROGER** *slaps the hand.)*

ROGER. G'wan home! G'wan home.

CARLYLE. You gonna hear from me.

(And he is gone out the door and down the hallway.)

ROGER. *(closing the door)* I can – and do – believe – that.

(RICHIE, *putting on his T-shirt, watches* **ROGER,** *who stubs out his cigarette, then crosses to the trash can to empty the ashtray, along the way picking up the calender page tossed by* **CARLYLE.)**

RICHIE. Who was that?

ROGER. Man's new, Rich. Dunno his name more than that "Carlyle" he said. He's new – just outa basic.

RICHIE. *(powdering under his arms, his stomach)* Oh, my God –

(As **BILLY** *returns, pushing a mop bucket with a wringer attached and carrying a container of wax.)*

ROGER. Me and Billy's gonna straighten up the area. You wanna help?

RICHIE. Sure, sure; help, help.

BILLY. *(talking to* **ROGER,** *but watching* **RICHIE,** *who is still putting powder under his arms)* I hadda steal the wax from Third Platoon.

ROGER. Good man.

BILLY. What? Whata you doin', singin'? *(moving to* **RICHIE,** *joking, offering some friendly advice)* Look at that, Rog. He's got enough jazz there for an entire beauty parlor. *(taking the can from* **RICHIE)** What is this? Baby powder! Baby powder!

RICHIE. I get rashes.

BILLY. Okay, okay, you get rashes, so what? They got powder for rashes that isn't baby powder. *(turning to check with* **ROGER)**

RICHIE. It doesn't work as good; I've tried it. Have you tried it? *(He towel-snaps* **BILLY.)**

BILLY. Man, I wish you could get yourself straight. *(He walks away from* **RICHIE.)** I'll mop, too, Roger – okay? Then I'll put down the wax and you can spread it? *(grabbing the second mop)*

RICHIE. What about buffing?

ROGER. In the morning. *(already busy mopping up near the door)*

RICHIE. What do you want me to do?

BILLY. *(heading to the opposite side of the room to work)* Get inside your locker and shut the door and don't holler for help. Nobody'll know you're there; you'll stay there.

RICHIE. But I'm so pretty.

BILLY. Now! *(pointing to* **ROGER***)* Tell that man you mean what you're sayin' Richie.

RICHIE. Mean what?

BILLY. That you really think you're pretty.

RICHIE. Of course I do; I am. Don't you think I am? Don't you think I am, Roger?

ROGER. I tole you – you fulla shit and you cute, man. Carlyle just tole you you cute, too.

RICHIE. Don't you think it's true, Billy?

BILLY. It's like I tole you, Rog.

RICHIE. What did you tell him?

BILLY. That you go down; that you go up and down like a yo-yo and you go blowin' all the trees like the wind.

*(***RICHIE*** is stunned. He looks at* **ROGER***, and then he turns and stares into his own locker. The others keep mopping.* **RICHIE** *takes out a towel, and putting it around his neck, he walks to where* **BILLY** *is working.)*

RICHIE. What the hell made you tell him I been down, Billy?

BILLY. *(still mopping)* It's in your eyes; I seen it.

RICHIE. What?

BILLY. You.

RICHIE. What is it, Billy, you think you're trying to say? You and all your wit and intelligence – your HUMANITY.

BILLY. I said it, Rich. I said what I was tryin' to say.

RICHIE. DID you?

BILLY. I think I did.

RICHIE. DO you?

BILLY. Loud and clear, baby. *(still mopping)*

ROGER. They got to put me in with the weirdos. Why is that, huh? How come the army HATE me – do this shit to me – KNOW what to do to me. *(whimsical, and then suddenly loud, angry)* Now you guys put socks in your mouths, right now – get shut up – or I am gonna beat you to death with each other. Roger got work to be do. To be doin' it!

RICHIE. *(returning to his bunk, he sits on his footlocker)* Roger, I think you're so innocent sometimes. Honestly, it's not such a terrible thing. Is it, Billy?

BILLY. How would I know? *(and then, realzing the implication, he slams his mop into the bucket)* Oh, go fuck yourself.

RICHIE. Well, I can give it a try, if that's what you want. Can I think of you as I do?

BILLY. *(throwing down his mop)* GODDAMNIT! That's it! IT!

(**BILLY** *storms straight over to* **RICHIE** *who still sit on his footlocker*)

Now I am gonna level with you. Are you gonna listen? You gonna hear what I say, Rich, and not what you think I'm saying'?

(**RICHIE** *turns away as if to rise, flippant and disdainful.*)

No! Don't get cute; don't turn away cute. I wanna say somethin' straight out to you, and I want you to hear it!

RICHIE. I'm all ears, goddamnit! For what, however, I do not know, except some boring evasion.

BILLY. At least wait the hell till you hear me!

RICHIE. *(irritated)* Okay, okay! What?

BILLY. Now this is level, Rich; this is straight talk. *(He is quiet, intense, seeking the exactly appropriate words.)* No B.S. No tricks. What you do on the side, that's your business, and I don't care about it. But if you don't cut the cute shit with me, I'm gonna turn you off. Completely. You

ain't gonna get a good mornin' outa me, you understand? Because it's getting' bad around here. I mean,
I know how you think – how you keep lookin' out
and seein' yourself, and that's what I'm tryin to tell
you because that's all that's happenin' Rich. That's
all there is to it when you look out at me and think
there's some kind of approval or whatever you see in
my eyes – you're just seein' yourself. And I'm talkin'
the simple quiet truth to you, Rich, I swear I am. –

(BILLY *walks away from* RICHIE *now and tries to go
back to the mopping. The moment is embarrassing for
them all.* ROGER *has watched, has tried to keep working.* RICHIE *flops back on his bunk and lays there.
There is silence.*)

RICHIE. How – do – you want me to be? I don't know how
else to be? (*honestly wishing he might be told*)

BILLY. Ohhh, man, that ain't any part of it.

RICHIE. Well, I don't come from the same kind of world as
you do.

BILLY. Damn, Richie, you think Roger and I come off the
same street?

ROGER. Shit –

RICHIE. All right. Okay. But I've just done what I wanted
all my life. If I wanted to do something, I just did it.
Honestly, I've never had to work or anything like that,
and I've always had nice clothing and money for cab
fare. Money for whatever I wanted. Always. I'm not like
you are.

(BILLY *has stopped mopping now and is seated on his
bunk facing* ROGER *and* RICHIE.)

ROGER. You ain't sayin you really done that stuff, though,
Rich.

RICHIE. What?

ROGER. That fag stuff.

RICHIE. (*He continues to look at* ROGER, *and then he looks
away.*) Yes.

ROGER. Do you even know what you're sayin' Richie? Do you even know what it means to be a fag?

RICHIE. Roger, of course I know what it is. I just told you I've done it. I thought you black people were supposed to understand all about suffering and human strangeness. I thought you had depth and vision from all your suffering. Has someone been misleading me? I just told you I did it. I know all about it. Everything. All the various positions.

ROGER. Yeh, so maybe you think you've tried it, but that don't make you it. I mean, we used to – in the old neighborhood, man, we had a couple dudes swung that way. But they was weird, man. There was this one little fella, he was a screamin' goddamn faggot – uh – *(considering* **RICHIE***)* Ohhh, ohhh, you ain't no screamin' goddamn faggot, Richie, no matter what you say. And the baddest man on the block was my boy Jerry Lemon. So one day Jerry's got the faggot in one a them ole deserted stairways, and he's bouncin' him off the walls. I'm just a little fella, see, and I'm watchin' the baddest man on the block do his thing. So he come bouncin' back into me, instead of Jerry, and just when he hit, he gave his ass this little twitch, man, like he thought he was gonna turn me on. I'd never a thought that was possible, man, for a man to be twitchin' his ass on me, just like he thought he was a broad. Scared me to death. I took off runnin'. Oh, oh, that ole neighborhood put me into all kinds a crap. I did some sufferin', just like Richie says. Like this once, I'm swingin' on up the street after school, and outa this phone booth comes this man with a goddamned knife stickin' outa his gut. So he sees me and starts tryin' to pull his motherfuckin' coat out over the handle, like he's worried about how he looks, man. "I didn't know this was gonna happen," he says. And then he falls over. He was just all of a sudden dead, man; just all of a sudden dead. You ever seen anything like that, Billy? Any crap like that?

(BILLY, sitting on ROGER's bunk, is staring at ROGER.)

BILLY. You really seen that?

ROGER. Richie's a big-city boy.

RICHIE. Oh, no; never anything like that.

ROGER. "Momma, help me," I am screamin'. "Jesus, Momma, help me." Little fella, he don't know how to act, he sees somethin' like that.

(For a moment, they are quiet, motionless, each alone with his thoughts.)

BILLY. How long you think we got?

ROGER. What do you mean? *(hanging up the mops)*

BILLY. Till they pack us up, man, ship us out.

ROGER. To the war, you mean? To Disneyland? Man, I dunno; that up to them IBMs. Them machines is figurin' that. Maybe tomorrow, maybe next week, maybe never.

RICHIE. I was reading they're planning to build it all up to more than five hundred thousand men over there. Americans. And they're going to keep it that way until they win.

BILLY. Be a great place to come back from, man, you know? I keep thinkin' about that. To have gone there, to have been there, to have seen it and lived.

ROGER. Well, what we got right here is a fool, gonna probably be one a them five hundred thousand, too.

(Retrieving a pack of cigarettes from his foot locker, ROGER lights up and sits on BILLY's bunk.)

ROGER. Do you know I cry at the goddamn anthem yet sometimes? The flag is flyin' at a ball game, the ole Roger gets all wet in the eye. After all the shit been done to his black ass. But I don't know what I think about this war. I do not know.

BILLY. I'm tellin' you, Rog – I've been doin' a lot of readin' and I think it's right we go. I mean, it's just like when North Korea invaded South Korea or when Hitler invaded Poland and all those other countries. He just kept testin' everybody and when nobody said no to him, he got so committed he couldn't back out even if he wanted. And that's what this Ho Chi Mihn is doin'. And all these other Communists. If we let 'em know somebody is gonna stand up against 'em, they'll back off, just like Hitler would have.

ROGER. There is folks, you know, who are sayin' L.B.J. is the Hitler, and not ole Ho Chi Mihn at all.

(**BILLY** *and* **ROGER** *have ended up facing each other, talking intently as if* **RICHIE** *is no longer in the room.*)

RICHIE. Well, I don't know anything about all that, but I am certain I don't want to go – whatever is going on. *(as if telling a ghost story)* I mean, those Vietcong don't just shoot you and blow you up, you know. My God, they've got these other awful things they do; putting elephant shit on these stakes in the ground, and then you step on em, and you got elephant shit in a wound on your foot. The infection is horrendous. And then there's these caves they hide in and when you go in after 'em, they've got these snakes that they've tied by their tails to the ceiling. So it's dark and the snake is furious from having been hung by its tail, and you crawl right into them – your face. My God.

BILLY. They do not. *(aware that* **ROGER** *knows what he said about snakes.)*

RICHIE. I read it Billy. They do.

BILLY. *(completely facetious)* That's bullshit, Richie.

ROGER. That's right, Richie. They maybe do that stuff with the elephant shit, but nobody's gonna tie a snake by it's tail, let ole Billy walk into it.

BILLY. That's disgusting, man.

ROGER. Guess you better get ready for the Klondike, my man.

BILLY. That is probably the most disgusting thing I ever heard of. I DO NOT WANT TO GO! NOT NOWHERE WHERE THAT KINDA SHIT IS GOIN' ON! L.B.J. is Hitler; suddenly I see it all very clearly.

ROGER. Billy got him a hatred for snakes.

RICHIE. I hate them, too. They're hideous.

BILLY. *(satirizing himself, perhaps in the manner of a politician)* I mean, that is one of the most awful things I ever heard of any person doing. I mean, any person who would hang a snake by it's tail in the dark of a cave in hope that some other person might crawl into it and get bitten to death, that first person is somebody who oughta be shot. And I hope that five hundred thousand other guys that get sent over there kill'em all–all them gooks–get 'em all driven back into Germany, where they belong. And in the meantime, I'll be holding the northern border against the snowmen. *(snapping to attention)*

ROGER. *(rising)* And in the meantime, before that, we better be getting' at the ole area here. Got to be strike troopers.

BILLY. Right.

RICHIE. Can I help?

ROGER. Sure. Be good.

(And he crosses to his footlocker and takes out a radio.)

ROGER. Think maybe I put on a little music, though it's gettin' late. We got time. Billy, you think?

BILLY. Sure.

ROGER. Sure. All right. We can be doin' it to the music.

(He plugs the radio into the floor outlet as **BILLY** *bolts for the door.)*

BILLY. I gotta go pee.

ROGER. You watch out for the snakes.

BILLY. It's the snowmen, man; the snowmen.

*(***BILLY*** is gone. A song comes from the radio. For a moment,* **ROGER** *watches* **RICHIE** *move about the room, carefully pouring wax onto the floor, trying to do it right.)*

RICHIE. How come you and Billy take all this so seriously, you know?

ROGER. What?

RICHIE. This army nonsense. *(He finds it tedious and a little disheartening; he really doesn't get it.)* You're always shining your brass and keeping your footlocker neat and your locker so neat. There's no point to any of it.

ROGER. We here, ain't we, Richie? We in the army. *(leisurely starting to spread the wax)*

RICHIE. There's no point to any of it. And doing those push-ups, the two of you.

(RICHIE gives up, setting the wax on his footlocker and flopping down onto his bunk, as ROGER continues to spread the wax.)

ROGER. We just see a lot of things the same way, is all. Army ought to be a serious business, even if sometimes it ain't.

RICHIE. You're lucky, you know, the two of you. Having each other for friends the way you do. I never had that kind of friend ever. Not even when I was little.

(For a quiet moment, ROGER works the mop, sort of peeking at RICHIE every now and then.)

ROGER. You ain't really inta that stuff, are you, Richie? *(It is a question that is a statement.)*

RICHIE. *(coyly)* What stuff is that, Roger?

ROGER. That fag stuff, man. You know. You ain't really into it, are you? You maybe messed in it a little is all – am I right?

RICHIE. I'm very weak, Roger. And by that I simply mean that if I have an impulse to do something, I don't know how to deny myself. If I feel like doing something, I just do it. I...will...admit to sometimes wishing I... was a little more like you and Billy, even, but not to any severe extent.

ROGER. But that's such a bad scene, Rich. You don't want that. Nobody wants that. Nobody wants to be a punk. Not nobody. You wanna know what I think it is? You just got in with the wrong bunch. Am I right? You just got in with a bad bunch. That can happen. And that's what I think happened to you. I bet you never had a chance to really run with the boys before. I mean, regular normal guys like Billy and me. How'd you come in the army, huh, Richie? You didn't get drafted, did you. You R.A. man.

(Having stopped working, **ROGER** *leans on the mop, looking at* **RICHIE.***)*

RICHIE. I know.

ROGER. That's my point. See!

RICHIE. About four years ago, I went to this party. I was very young, and I went to this party with a friend who was older and – this "fag stuff" as you call it, was going on – so I did it.

ROGER. And then you come in the army to get away from it, right? Huh?

RICHIE. I don't know.

ROGER. Sure.

RICHIE. I don't know, Roger.

ROGER. Sure; sure. And now you're getting' a chance to run with the boys for a little, you'll get yourself straightened around. I know it for a fact; I know that thing.

(From off there is the sudden loud bellowing sound of **SERGEANT ROONEY.***)*

ROONEY. THERE AIN'T BEEN NO SOLDIERS IN THIS CAMP BUT ME. I BEEN THE ONLY ONE – I BEEN THE ONLY ME!

*(***BILLY** *comes dashing into the room.)*

BILLY. Oh, boy.

ROGER. Guess who?

ROONEY. FOR SO LONG I BEEN THE ONLY GODDAMN ONE!

*(***RICHIE** *tries to get under his sheets while* **ROGER** *scurries to put the wax away.)*

BILLY. Hut who hee whor! He's got some yo-yo with him, Rog!

ROGER. Huh?

(**BILLY, ROGER** *and* **RICHIE** *all hurry into their bunks just as* **SERGEANT COKES** *and* **SERGEANT ROONEY** *stride in. Both are in fatigues and big-bellied and drunk. They are in their fifties, their hair whitish and cut short. Both men carry whiskey bottles, beer bottles.* **COKES** *is a little neater than* **ROONEY,** *and he wears jungle fatigues and canvas-sided jungle boots.* **ROONEY,** *very disheveled, chomps on the stub of a big cigar. They swagger in, looking for fun, and stand there side by side.*)

ROONEY. What kinda platoon I got here? You buncha shit sacks. Everybody look sharp. Off and on!

(*The three boys lie there, unmoving.*)

COKES. OFF AND ON!

ROGER. (*sitting up*) What's happenin', Sergeant?

ROONEY. Shut up, Moore! You want a belt?

(*Shoving his bottle of whiskey at* **ROGER,** *he spills a little on* **ROGER,** *who takes the bottle.*)

ROGER. How can I say no?

COKES. My name is Cokes!

BILLY. (*eyeing the whiskey, rising to sit on the side of his bunk*) How about me, too?

COKES. You wait your turn.

(**ROONEY** *gapes at the three boys, as if they are fools, and then he indicates* **COKES.**)

ROGER. Don't you see what I got here?

BILLY. Who do I follow for my turn?

ROONEY. (*suddenly indignant*) Don't you see what I got here? Everybody on their feet and at attention! (*as the boys hesitate*) I MEAN IT!

(**RICHIE** *bounds to his feet as* **BILLY** *and* **ROGER** *climb from their bunks and all three stand at attention along the front of* **ROGER** *and* **BILLY**'s *bunks.*)

ROONEY. This here is my friend, who in addition just come back from the war! The goddamn war! He been to it and he come back! *(like a Drill Instructor, with* **COKES** *as the prime example of his very important lesson)* The man's a fuckin' hero! He's always been a fuckin' hero.

COKES. No-o-o-o-o-o... *(a little embarrassed, taking a drink)*

ROONEY. Show 'em your boots, Cokes. Show 'em your jungle boots.

*(***ROONEY*** moves to* **COKES**, *urging him toward* **RICH-IE**'s *footlocker, and he sees that the boys are facing front.)*

RIGHT FACE!

(The boys turn as ordered. They are now aimed at **RICH-IE**'s *locker, as* **ROONEY** *lifts one of* **COKES**'s *feet onto the foot locker, displaying it for the boys.)*

ROONEY. Lookee that boot. That ain't no everyday goddamn army boot. That is a goddamn jungle boot! That green canvas is a jungle boot 'cause a the heat, and them little holes in the bottom are so the water can run out when you been walkin' in a lotta water like in a jungle swamp. *(sly and proud, he gives the boys a look)* The army ain't no goddamn fool. You see a man wearin' boots like that, you might as well see he's got a chestful a medals, 'cause he been to the war. He don't have no boots like that unless he been to the war! Which is where I'm goin' and all you slaphappy motherfuckers, too. Got to go kill some gooks. *(nodding at them, smiling)* That's right.

COKES. Gonna piss on 'em. Old booze. 'At's what I did. Piss in the rivers. Goddamn GI's secret weapon is old booze and he's pissin' it in all their runnin' water. Makes 'em yellow. Ahhhha ha, ha, ha! *(laughing at his own joke as* **ROONEY** *joins him)*

ROONEY. Me and Cokesy been in so much shit together we oughta be brown. *(Catching himself, he looks at* **ROGER**.*)* Don't take no offense at that, Moore. We been swimmin' in it. One Hundred and First Airborne, together. One-oh-one. Screamin' goddamn Eagles!

(Facing each other, eyes glinting, they make sudden loud screaming-eagle sounds.)

ROONEY. This ain't the army; you punks ain't in the army. You ain't ever seen the army. The army is Airborne! Airborne!

COKES. *(beginning to stomp his feet)* Airborne, Airborne! ALL THE WAY!

(As RICHIE, *amused and hoping for a drink, too, reaches out toward* ROONEY.*)*

RICHIE. Sergeant, Sergeant, I can have a little drink, too.

ROONEY. *(Though he hands the bottle to* RICHIE, *he stares at him, as if puzzled.)* Are you kiddin' me? You gotta be kiddin' me. *(he looks to* ROGER*)* He's kiddin' me, ain't he, Moore? *(he looks to* COKES*)* Ain't he, Cokesy?

*(*COKES *steps forward, retrieving the bottle and taking charge for his bewildered friend.)*

COKES. Don't you know you are takin' booze from the hand a the future goddamn Congressional Medal of Honor winner medal – ? *(He beams at* ROONEY.*)* Ole Rooney, Ole Rooney. *(giving* ROONEY *a bear hug)* He almost done it already.

(And ROONEY *starts screaming "Aggggggghhhhhhhhh," their screaming-eagle sound, and making clawing eagle gestures at the air. He stomps his feet.* COKES *instantly joins in, stomping yelling.)*

ROONEY. Let's show these shit sacks how men are men jumpin' outa planes. Aggggggghhhhhhhhh.

(Stomping and yelling, they make a gesture as if hooking up their rip cords inside the plane.)

ROONEY. A plane fulla yellin' stompin' men!

(Like paratroopers in a a plane, stomping toward the door, ROONEY *followed by* COKES, *they move along, making eagle sounds.)*

COKES. All yellin' stompin' men!

(They yell louder and louder as **ROONEY** *leaps up on* **BILLY***'s bunk and runs the length of it until he is on the footlocker, while* **COKES** *is still on the floor, stomping. And* **ROONEY** *leaps into the air, yelling, "GERONIMO-O O-O!" As* **COKES** *leaps onto the locker and then into the air bellowing, "GERONIMO-O-O-O!" They stand side by side, their arms held up in the air as if grasping the shroud lines of open chutes. They seem to float there in silence.)*

COKES. What a feelin' –

ROONEY. Beautiful feelin' –

(For a moment they float, adrift in the room, the sky, their memory. **COKES** *smiles at* **ROONEY***.)*

COKES. Remember that one guy, O'Flannigan – ?

ROONEY. *(nodding, smiling)* O'Flannigan –

COKES. He was this one guy – O'Flannigan –

(He moves now toward **BILLY**, **ROGER** *and* **RICHIE**, *who have broken ranks and gathered on* **ROGER***'s bunk and footlocker.* **ROONEY** *follows a step, then drifts back to* **RICHIE***'s bunk, where he sits and then lies back, listening.)*

ROONEY. We was testing chutes where you could just pull a lever by your ribs here when you hit the ground – see – and the chute would come off you, because it was just after a whole bunch a guys had been dragged to death in an unexpected and terrible wind at Fort Bragg. So they wanted you to be able to release the chute when you hit if there was a bad wind when you hit. So O'Flannigan was this kinda joker who had the goddamn sense a humor of a clown and nerves, I tell you, of steel, and he says he's gonna release the lever midair, then reach up, grab the lines and float on down, hanging. *(With one hand he casually demonstrates.)* So I seen him pull the lever at five hundred feet and he reaches up to two fistfuls a air – *(His hands paw at the air above his head, seeking lines that are not there.)* – the chute's twenty feet above him, and he went into the ground like a knife.

BILLY. Geezus.

ROONEY. *(nodding gently)* Didn't get to sing the song, I bet.

COKES. *(standing, staring at the ground)* No way.

RICHIE. What song?

ROONEY. *(surging, furious)* Shit sack! Shit sack!

RICHIE. What song, Sergeant Rooney?

ROONEY. "Beautiful Streamer," shit sack. *(flopping back down)*

COKES. *(staring skyward in another reverie)* I saw this one guy – never forget it. Never. This guy with his chute goin' straight up above him in a streamer, like a tulip, only white, you know. All twisted and never gonna open. Like a big icicle sticking straight up above him. He went right by me. We met eyes, sort of. He was lookin' real puzzled. He looks right at me. Then he looks up in the air at the chute, then down at the ground.

ROONEY. Did he sing it?

COKES. He didn't sing it. He started going like this.

(He reaches upward with both hands and begins to claw at the sky desperately while his legs pump up and down.)

COKES. Like he was gonna climb right up the air.

RICHIE. Ohhhhh, Geezus.

BILLY. God.

*(**ROONEY** suddenly sits up on **RICHIE**'s bunk.)*

ROONEY. Cokes got the Silver Star for rollin' a barrel a oil down a hill in Korea into forty-seven chinky Chinese gooks who were climbin' up the hill and when he shot into it with his machine gun, it blew them all to grape jelly.

*(**COKES**, rocking a little on his feet, begins to hum and then sing "Beautiful Streamer," to the tune of Stephen Foster's "Beautiful Dreamer.")*

COKES. "Beautiful streamer, open for me – The sky is above me – " *(the singing fades)* But the one I remember is this little guy in his spider hole, which is a hole in the ground with a lid over it. *(As if* **BILLY** *'s footlocker before him is the spider hole, he has fixed on it, is moving toward it)* And he shot me in the ass as I was runnin' by, but the bullet hit me so hard – it knocked me into this ditch where he couldn't see me. I got behind him. *(approaching* **BILLY** *'s footlocker)* Crawlin'. And I dropped a grenade into his hole.

(He jams a whiskey bottle into the footlocker, then slams down the lid and sits on it.)

COKES. Then sat on the lid, him bouncin' and yellin' under me. Bouncin' and yellin' under the lid. I could hear him. Feel him. I just sat there.

(Silence. **ROONEY** *waits, then leans forward.)*

ROONEY. He was probably singin' it.

COKES. *(sitting there)* I think so.

ROONEY. You think we should let 'em hear it?

BILLY. We're good boys. We're good ole boys.

COKES. *(standing)* I don't care who hears it, I just wanna be singin' it.

*(***ROONEY*** *rises and goes to the boys, speaking carefully, as if lecturing on a matter of great importance.)*

ROONEY. You listen up; you just be listenin' up, 'cause if you hear it right you can maybe stop bein' shit sacks. This is what a man sings, he's goin' down through the air, his chute don't open.

*(***ROONEY*** *joins* ***COKES*** *and together they sing.)*

ROONEY & COKES. *(singing)* Beautiful streamer,
　　Open for me,
　　The sky is above me,
　　But no canopy.

BILLY. *(murmuring)* I don't believe it.

ROONEY & COKES. Counted ten thousand,
　　　Pulled on the cord.
　　　My chute didn't open,
　　　I shouted, "Dear Lord."
　　　Beautiful streamer,
　　　This looks like the end,
　　　The earth is below me,
　　　My body won't bend.
　　　Just like a mother
　　　Watching o'er me
　　　Beautiful streamer,
　　　Ohhhhh, open for me.

ROGER. Un-fuckin'-believable.

ROONEY. *(beaming with pride)* Ain't that a beauty.

　　*(***COKES*** *topples forward, collapsing to the floor. The three
　　boys leap to their feet.* ***ROONEY*** *lunges towards* ***COKES***.*)*

RICHIE. Sergeant!

BILLY. Jesus!

ROGER. Hey!

ROONEY. Cokie! Cokie!

COKES. Huh? Huh?

　　(He sits up to find ***ROONEY*** *kneeling beside him.)*

ROONEY. Jesus, Cokie.

COKES. I been doin' that; I been doin' that. It don't mean
　　nothin'.

ROONEY. No, no.

COKES. *(as* ***ROONEY*** *helps him get back to his feet)* I told 'em
　　when they wanted to send me back I ain't got no prob-
　　lem with my heart; they wanna check it. They think I
　　got it. I don't think I got it. Rooney? Whata you think?

ROONEY. No.

COKES. My mother had it. She had it. Just 'cause she did
　　and I been fallin' down.

ROONEY. It don't mean nothin'.

COKES. I tole 'em I fall down 'cause I'm drunk. I'm drunk all the time.

ROONEY. You'll be goin' back over there with me, is what I know, Cokie. *(patting* COKES, *nodding, dusting him off)* That is what I know.

*(*BILLY *comes up to them, daring to pat* COKES *on the back.)*

BILLY. That was somethin', Sergeant Cokes. Jesus.

*(*ROONEY *whirls on him, ferocious, pushing him away.)*

ROONEY. Get the fuck away, Wilson! Whata you know?! Get the fuck away! You don't know shit. Get away! You don't know shit.

*(*BILLY *backs away and when he is far enough,* ROONEY *turns to* COKES, *who is standing on his own now.)*

ROONEY. Me and Cokes are going' to the war zone like we oughta. Gonna blow it to shit.

(And they are both laughing, as ROONEY *whirls on the boys.)*

ROONEY. Ohhh, I'm gonna be so happy to be away from you assholes; you pussies. Not one regular army people among you possible. I swear it to my mother who is holy. You just be watching the papers for Cokes and Rooney doin' darin' brave deeds. Cause' we're old hands at it. Makin' shit disappear. Goddamn wooosh!

COKES. Whhooosh!

ROONEY. Demnalitions. Me and… *(knowing he mispronouced)* Me and Cokie…Demnal… Demnali…

RICHIE. You can do it, Sergeant.

BILLY. Get it.

ROGER. Cause' you're cool with dynamite, is what you're tryin' to say.

ROONEY. *(charging at* ROGER, *bellowing)* Shut the fuck up, that's what you can do; and go to goddamn sleep. You buncha shit…sacks. Buncha mothers – know-it-all motherin' shit sacks – that's what you are.

COKES. *(taking charge)* Just goin' to sleep is what you can do, cause Rooney and me fought it through two wars already and we can make it through this one more and this heart attack crap-ola that comes or doesn't come – who gives a shit? Not guys like us. We're goin' just pretty as pie. And it's lights-out time, ain't it, Rooney?

ROONEY. Past it, goddamnit. So the lights are goin' out!

(BILLY, RICHIE and ROGER rush to their wall lockers, where they strip to their underwear, preparing for bed.)

ROONEY. *(pacing the room, glaring)* Somebody's gotta teach you soldierin'. You hear me? Or you wanna go outside and march around awhile, huh? We can do that if you wanna. Huh? You tell me? Marchin' or sleepin'? What's it gonna be?

RICHIE. *(hurrying to his bunk)* Flick out the ole lights, Sergeant; that's what we say.

BILLY. *(climbing into his bed)* Put out the ole lights.

ROGER. *(pulling up the covers)* Do it.

COKES. SHUT UP *(doing his best to stand at attention)* And that's an order. Just shut up! I got grenades down the hall. I got a pistol. I know where to get nitro. You don't shut up, I'll blow...you...to...fuck.

(Making a military left-face, he stalks to the wall switch and turns the lights out. ROONEY is watching proudly, as COKES faces the boys again in the now darkened room.)

COKES. That's right.

(With only a spill of light from the hall coming in the open door, COKES and ROONEY walk out, leaving the door partly open. Then they are visible through the windows as they go along the walkway outside the back wall.)

COKES. *(on the walkway)* What you wanna do?

ROONEY. *(on the walkway)* I dunno. But I ain't sleepy.

COKES. *(on the walkway)* I ain't sleepy.

(And then the SERGEANTS are gone. RICHIE, ROGER, and BILLY lie in their bunks, staring, motionless in the sudden quiet. Light touches each of them as they lie there.)

ROGER. Lord have mercy, if that ain't a pair. If that ain't one pair a beauties.

BILLY. Oh, yeah.

ROGER. Too much, man – too, too much.

RICHIE. They made me sad; but I loved them, sort of. Better than the movies.

ROGER. Too much. Too, too much.

(silence)

BILLY. What time is it?

ROGER. Sleep time, man. Sleep time.

(silence)

BILLY. Right.

ROGER. They were somethin'. Too much.

BILLY. Too much.

RICHIE. Night.

ROGER. Night. *(after a breath or two)* Night, Billy.

BILLY. Night.

(RICHIE stirs in his bunk, then settles. ROGER turns onto his side, his back to BILLY. BILLY is motionless. He lies on his back, his head propped up on the white of his pillow illuminated by the light coming in the middle window just behind him. As BILLY speaks, ROGER and RICHIE listen without moving.)

BILLY. I – had a buddy, Rog – and this is the whole thing, this is the whole point – a kid I grew up with, played ball with in high school, and he was a tough little cat, a real bad man sometimes. Used to have gangster pictures up in his room. Anyway, we got into this deal where we'd drive on down to the big city, man, you know, hit the bad spots, let some queer pick us up – sort of – long enough to buy us some good stuff. It was kinda the thing to do for a while, and we all did it, the whole gang of us. So we'd let these cats pick us up, most of 'em old guys, and they were hurtin' and happy as hell to have us, and we'd get a lot of free booze, maybe a meal, and we'd turn 'em on. Then pretty soon they'd ask us did we want to go over to their place. Sure, we'd say, and order one more drink, and then when we hit the street, we'd tell 'em to kiss off, call them fag and queer and jazz like that and tell them to kiss off. And Frankie, the kid I'm tellin' you about, he had a mean streak in him and if they gave us a bad time at all, he'd put 'em down. That's the way he was. So that kinda jazz went on and on for sort of a long time and it was a good deal if we were low on cash or needed a laugh and it went on for a while. And then Frankie – one day he come up to me – and he says he was goin' home with the guy he was with. He said, what the hell, what did it matter? And he's sayin' – Frankie's sayin' – why don't I tag along? What the hell, he's sayin', what does it matter who does it to you, some broad or some old guy, you close your eyes, a mouth's a mouth, it don't matter – that's what he's sayin'. I tried to talk him out of it, but he wasn't hearin' anything I was sayin'. So the next day, see, he calls me up to tell me about it. Okay, okay, he says, it was a cool scene, he says; they played poker, a buck minimum, and he made a fortune. Frankie was eatin' it up, man. It was a pretty way to live, he says. So he stayed at it, and he had this nice little girl he was goin' with at the time. You know the way a real bad cat can sometimes do that – have a good little girl who's crazy about him and he is for her, too, and he's a different cat when he's with her?

ROGER. Uh-huh.

BILLY. Well, that was him and Linda, and then one day he dropped her, he cut her loose. He was hooked, man. He was into it, with no way he knew out – you understand what I'm sayin'? He had got his ass hooked. He had never thought he would and then one day he woke up and he was on it. He just hadn't been told, that's the way I figure it; somebody didn't tell him somethin'

he shoulda been told and he come to me wailin' one
day, man, all broke up and wailin', my boy Frankie, my
main man, and he was a fag. He was a faggot, black
Roger, and I'm not lyin'. I am not lyin' to you.

ROGER. Damn.

BILLY. So that's the whole thing, man; that's the whole
thing.

(Silence. They lie there.)

ROGER. Holy – Christ. Richie – you hear him? You hear
what he said?

RICHIE. He's a storyteller.

ROGER. What you mean?

RICHIE. I mean, he's a storyteller, all right; he tells stories,
all right.

ROGER. What are we into now? You wanna end up like that
friend a his, or you don't believe what he said? Which
are you sayin'?

*(The door swings open. They all startle and look to the
open door.)*

ROGER. Hey, hey, what's happenin'?

*(Imitative sounds of a machine gun, then explosions are
being made by someone at the door.)*

BILLY. Who's happenin'?

*(**CARLYLE**, drunk and playful, comes crawling in.
ROGER, **RICHIE**, and **BILLY** all see him.)*

ROGER. You attackin' or you retreatin', man?

CARLYLE. *(with a big grin)* Hey, baby – ?

*(He continues shooting, crawling. **BILLY**, **ROGER** and
RICHIE exchange questioning looks.)*

ROGER. What's happenin', man? Whatcha doin'?

CARLYLE. I dunno, soul; I dunno. Practicin' my duties, my
new abilities. *(flopping onto his side, crawling again)* The
low crawl, man; like I was taught in basic, that's what
I'm doin'. You gotta know your shit, man, else you get

your ass blown so far away you don't ever see it again.
Oh, sure, you guys don't care. I know it. You got it
made. You got it made. I don't got it made. You got
a little home here, got friends, people to talk to. I got
nothin'. You got jobs they probably ain't ever gonna
ship you out, you got so important jobs. I got no job.
They don't even wanna give me a job. I know it. They
are gonna kill me. They are gonna send me over there
to get me killed, goddammit. WHATSAMATTER
WITH ALL YOU PEOPLE?

(The exploding anger is mixed with grieving, and
ROGER *hurries over to* **CARLYLE.** *)*

ROGER. *(gently, firmly)* Hey, man, get cool, get some cool;
purchase some cool, man.

CARLYLE. Awwww – *(clumsily, turning away)*

ROGER. Just hang in there.

CARLYLE. I don't wanna be no dead man. I don't wanna
be the one they all thinkin' is so stupid he's the only
one'll go, they tell him; they don't even have to give
him a job. I got thoughts, man, in my head; alla time,
burnin', burnin' thoughts a understandin'.

ROGER. Don't you think we know that, man? It ain't the
way you're sayin' it.

CARLYLE. It is.

ROGER. No. I mean, we all probably gonna go. We all probably gonna have to go.

CARLYLE. No-o-o-o-o.

ROGER. I mean it.

CARLYLE. *(He nearly topples over.)* I am very drunk. *(steadying
himelf, he looks at* **ROGER***)* You think so?

ROGER. I'm sayin' so. And I am sayin', "No sweat." No
point.

CARLYLE. Awwwww, dammit, dammit, mother – shit – it –
ohhhhhhh. *(lyng down to the floor, the rage and anguish
softening)* I mean it. I mean it.

(Silence. He lies there, almost peaceful, almost asleep.)

ROGER. What – a you doin' – ?

CARLYLE. Huh?

ROGER. I don't know what you're up to on our freshly mopped floor.

CARLYLE. Gonna go sleep – okay? No sweat – *(very polite, as he peers up)* Can I, soul? Izzit all right?

ROGER. Sure, man, sure, if you wanna, but why don't you go where you got a bed? Don't you like beds?

CARLYLE. Dunno where's zat. *(so sad, so lost)* My bed. I can' fin' it. I can' fin' my own bed. I looked all over, but I can' fin' it anywhere. GONE!

(Settling back down, he squirms to make a nest and hugs his bottle.)

ROGER. Okay, okay, man. *(grabbing the blanket from his bunk)* But get on top a this, man. *(spreading the blanket)* Make it softer. C'mon, c'mon – get on this.

(BILLY is moving now to hand his blanket to ROGER, who adds it to CARLYLE's little camp site on the floor.)

BILLY. Cat's hurtin', Rog.

ROGER. Ohhhh, yeh.

CARLYLE. Ohhhhh – it was so sweet at home – it was so sweet, baby; so-o-o good. They doin' dances make you wanna cry –

(Hugging the blankets now, he drifts in a kind of dream.)

ROGER. I know, man.

CARLYLE. So sweet – !

(BILLY is moving back to his own bunk.)

ROGER. I know, man.

CARLYLE. So sweet – !

ROGER. Yeh.

CARLYLE. How come I gotta be here?

(On his way to close the door, ROGER falters.)

ROGER. I dunno, Jim.

(BILLY is watching from his bed, as ROGER gently closes the door and starts back toward his bunk.)

BILLY. I know why he's gotta be here, Roger. You wanna know? Why don't you ask me?

ROGER. Okay. How come he gotta be here?

BILLY. *(smiling)* Freedom's frontier, man. That's why.

ROGER. *(settling on the edge of his bunk)* Oh – yeh...

(As a distant bugle begins to play taps, RICHIE, carrying a blanket, is approaching CARLYLE. ROGER lays back in his bunk. BILLY is watching RICHIE place the blanket over CARLYLE, who does not stir as the bugle plays on.)

ROGER. Bet that ole sarge don't live a year, Billy. Fuckin' blow his own ass sky high.

(Having covered CARLYLE, RICHIE straightens in order to return to his bunk.)

BILLY. *(whispering)* Richie – !

(RICHIE hesitates and stands, and then moves to his bed.)

BILLY. Richie – how come you gotta keep doin' that stuff?

(BILLY watches RICHIE climb into his bed.)

BILL. How come?

ROGER. He dunno, man. Do you? You dunno, do you, Rich?

RICHIE. No.

CARLYLE. *(from deep in sleep and longing)* It – was – so – pretty – !

RICHIE. No.

(The lights fade to black with the last soft notes of taps.)

End of Act One

ACT TWO

Scene One

(Music: Soldier Boy *sung by* The Shirelles *plays in the dark, and then the lights come up on the cadre room. It is late afternoon and* **BILLY** *is lying on his stomach, listening to the radio, his head at the foot of the bunk, his chin resting on his hands. He wears gym shorts and sweat socks; his T-shirt lies on the bunk and his sneakers are on the floor.* Soldier Boy *plays over* **BILLY** *for moment and then the quality transforms to a sound produced by the radio playing up by the back wall.* **ROGER** *comes in dressed in his khakis, headed for his locker.)*

ROGER. Hey.

(At the wall locker he takes out a basketball and sneakers and then, after placing his sneakers and basketball on his bunk, he heads for his footlocker)

BILLY. Rog – you think I'm a busybody? In any way?

(Silence. **ROGER** *removes socks from the footlocker and sits on his bunk, where he starts lacing his sneakers.)* Roger?

ROGER. Huh? Uh-uh.

BILLY. Some people do. I mean, back home. *(briefly, he looks at* **ROGER***)* Or that I didn't know how to behave. Sort of.

ROGER. It's time we maybe get changed, don't you think?

(He rises and goes to his locker, takes off his trousers, shoes and socks.)

BILLY. Yeh. I guess. I don't feel like it, though. I don't feel good, don't know why.

ROGER. Be good for you, man; be good for you. *(pulling on his gym shorts)*

BILLY. Yeh. *(thinking, staring off)* I mean, a lot a people thought like I didn't know how to behave in a simple way. You know? That I overcomplicated everything. I didn't think so. Don't think so. I just thought I was seein' complications that were there but nobody else saw. I mean, Wisconsin's a funny place. All those clear-eyed people sayin' "Hello" and lookin' you straight in the eye. Everybody's good, you think, and happy and honest. And then there's all of a sudden a neighbor who goes mad as a hatter. I had a neighbor who came out of his house one morning with axes in both hands. He started then attackin' the cars that were driving up and down in front of his house. An' we all knew why he did it, sorta.

(He pauses; he thinks, looks to **ROGER** *who is back at his bunk putting on his socks.)*

BILLY. It made me wanna be a priest. I wanted to be a priest then. I was sixteen. Priests could help people. Could take away what hurt 'em. I wanted that, I thought. Somethin', huh?

ROGER. *(spinning the basketball)* Yeh. But everybody's got feelin's like that sometimes.

BILLY. I don't know.

ROGER. You know, you oughta work on a little jump shot, my man. *(giving a little demonstation)* Get you some kinda fall-away jumper to go with that beauty of a hook. Make you tough out there.

BILLY. *(Sitting, he starts pulls on a T-shirt.)* Can't fuckin' do it. Not my game. I mean, like that bar we go to. You think I could get a job there bartendin', maybe? I could learn the ropes.

(as **ROGER** *walks to his locker)*

BILLY. You think I could get a job there off-duty hours?

ROGER. You don't want no job. It's that little black-haired waitress you wantin' to know.

BILLY. No, man. Not really.

ROGER. It's okay. She tough, man.

BILLY. I mean, not the way you're sayin' it, is all. Sure, there's somethin' about her. I don't know what. I ain't even spoke to her yet. But somethin'. I mean, what's she doin' there? When she's dancin', it's like she knows somethin'. She's degradin' herself, I sometimes feel. You think she is?

ROGER. Man, you don't even know the girl. She's workin'.

BILLY. I'd like to talk to her. Tell her stuff. Find out about her. Sometimes I'm thinkin' about her and it and I got a job there, I get to know her and she and I get to be real tight, man – close, you know. Maybe we screw, maybe we don't. It's nice – whatever.

ROGER. Sure. She a real fine-lookin' chippy, Billy. Got nice cakes. Nice little titties.

BILLY. I think she's smart, too.

(**ROGER** *cannot help but start laughing, and* **BILLY** *finds himself absurd and comical.*)

BILLY. Oh, all I do is talk. "Yabba-yabba." I mean, my mom and dad are really terrific people. How'd they ever end up with somebody so weird as me?

(**ROGER** *moves to him, jostles him.*)

ROGER. I'm tellin' you, the gym and a little ball is what you need. Little exercise. Little bumpin' into people. The soul is tellin' you.

BILLY. I mean, Roger, you remember how we met in P Company? Both of us brand-new. You started talkin' to me. You just started talkin' to me and you didn't stop.

ROGER. (*tossing the ball from hand to hand*) Yeh.

BILLY. Did you see somethin' in me made you pick me?

ROGER. I was talkin' to everybody, man. For that whole day. Two whole days. You was just the first one to talk back friendly. Though you didn't say much, as I recall.

BILLY. The first white person, you mean.

(**BILLY** *rises and goes to his locker, where he starts putting on his sweat clothes.*)

ROGER. Yeh. I was tryin' to come outa myself a little. Do like the fuckin' headshrinker been tellin' me to stop them fuckin' headaches I was havin', you know. Now let us do fifteen or twenty push-ups and get over to that gymnasium, like I been sayin'. Then we can take our civvies with us – we can shower and change at the gym.

BILLY. I don't know – I don't know what it is I'm feelin'. Sick like.

(**BILLY** *moves wearily, sagging as if he might fall back onto his bunk, but* **ROGER** *shoves him playfully forward, where they both fall into the push-up position, side by side.*)

ROGER. Do 'em, trooper. Do 'em. Get it.

(**ROGER** *starts.* **BILLY** *joins in.* **ROGER** *counts,* "One, two, three..." *At about five,* **ROGER** *realizes that* **BILLY** *has his knees on the floor, and gives him a disgusted look.* **BILLY** *admits his cheating with a grin, and they start again. This time,* **BILLY** *counts in double time. At about* "seven," **RICHIE** *enters behind them and neither* **BILLY** *nor* **ROGER** *see him.* **RICHIE** *watches them closely, wryly amused.*)

ROGER & BILLY. – seven, eight, nine, ten, eleven, twelve –

RICHIE. No, no; no, no; no, no, no. That's not it; that's not it.

(*They keep going, now yelling the numbers louder and louder as* **RICHIE** *crosses to his locker for a bottle of cologne.*)

ROGER & BILLY. ...TWELVE, THIRTEEN...

(*Returning closer,* **RICHIE** *watches, dabbing cologne on his face.*)

ROGER & BILLY. ...FOURTEEN, FIFTEEN....

RICHIE. You'll never get it like that. You're so far apart and you're both humping at the same time. And all that counting. It's so unromantic.

*(Bounding up, **ROGER** moves to his bunk to pick up the basketball.)*

ROGER. We was exercisin', Richard. You heard a that?

RICHIE. Call it what you will, Roger. Everybody has their own cute little pet names for it.

*(**ROGER** flips the ball to **BILLY**, who fires it at **RICHIE**.)*

BILLY. Hey!

*(Hitting **RICHIE** in the chest, the ball sends the cologne bottle flying. **RICHIE** yelps.)*

BILLY. You missed.

*(As **RICHIE** bends to pick up the cologne from the floor, **BILLY** retrieves the ball.)*

RICHIE. Billy, Billy, Billy, please, please, the ruffian approach will not work with me. It impresses me not even one tiny little bit. All you've done is spill my cologne.

BILLY. That was my aim.

*(Grabbing up his sweat shirt from the bunk, **BILLY** starts for the door. **ROGER**, having taken his suit bag of civilian clothes from his locker, follows along.)*

ROGER. See you.

*(As **BILLY** is passing, **RICHIE** sprays him with cologne, some of it getting on **ROGER**. **ROGER** and **BILLY**, groaning and cursing, rush out the door with **RICHIE** chasing them.)*

RICHIE. *(looking out after them, calling)* Try the more delicate approach next time, Bill.

*(**RICHIE** stands a moment, leaning against the frame. Then he scans the room and strolls to **BILLY**'s bunk, singing as he goes: "He's just my Bill, an ordinary guy...." Humming and singing a little more, he squirts cologne on **BILLY**'s pillow, then shrugs and goes to his locker,*

where he deposits the cologne, takes off his uniform shirt, shoes, and socks. In his T-shirt, he takes a hardcover copy of Pauline Kael's I Lost It at the Movies *and starts for his bunk. But instead he tosses the book onto his bed and stands over the sport where Billy and Roger did the pushups. He drops into the pushup position and does four or five sturdy pushups, counting them out and then he freezes. He lowers his knees to the floor.)*

RICHIE. Am I out of my fucking mind? Those two are crazy. I'm not crazy.

(He jumps up and strides to his locker. With an ashtray, matches, and a pack of cigarettes, he goes to his bunk and makes himself comfortable to read, his head propped up on a pillow. He opens the book, finds his place, thinks a little, starts to read, quickly interested. And then CARLYLE *steps into the room. He rushes in, looking at* ROGER's *bed and area, advancing several steps into the room before he even notices* RICHIE. *They stare at each other.)*

CARLYLE. *(extremely disappointed)* Ain't nobody here, man?

RICHIE. Hello, Carlyle. How are you today?

CARLYLE. Ain't nobody here? *(He is nervous and angrily disappointed.)*

RICHIE. Who do you want?

CARLYLE. Where's the black boy?

RICHIE. Roger? My God, why do you keep calling him that? Don't you know his name yet? Roger. *(thickening his voice at this imitating someone very stupid)* Roger.

(CARLYLE stares at him.)

CARLYLE. Yeh. Where is he?

RICHIE. I am not his keeper, you know. I am not his private secretary, you know.

CARLYLE. I do not know. I do not know. That is why I am asking. *(prowling to* ROGER's *area)* I come to see him. You are here. I ask you. I don't know. I mean, Carlyle made a fool outa himself comin' in here the other

night, talkin' on and on like how he did. Lay on the
floor. *(This is why he's here: to make sure no one thinks he's
that blubbering drunk.)* He remember. You remember?
It all one hype, man; that all one hype. You know what
I mean. *(sitting on* **ROGER***'s bed)* That ain't the real
Carlyle was in here. This one here and now the real
Carlyle. Who the real Richie?

RICHIE. Well – the real Richie – has gone home. To Man-
hattan. I, however, am about to read this book. *(which
he returns to)*

CARLYLE. Oh. Shit. Jus' you the only one here, then, huh?

RICHIE. So it would seem.

*(As he looks high in the air and then under the bunk as
if to find someone,* **CARLYLE**, *disgustedly, starts for the
door.)*

RICHIE. So it would seem. *(seeing that* **CARLYLE** *is leaving)*
Did you hear about Martin?

CARLYLE. *(stopping)* What happened to Martin? I ain't seen
him.

RICHIE. They are shipping him home. Someone told about
what he did to himself. I don't know who.

CARLYLE. Wasn't me. Not me. I keep that secret.

RICHIE. I'm sure you did.

(Rising, **RICHIE** *walks past* **CARLYLE** *to the door, cigarette pack in hand.)*

RICHIE. You want a cigarette? Or don't you smoke? Or do
you have to go right away? *(He closes the door.)* There's
a chill sometimes coming down the hall, I don't know
from where. *(Crossing back to his bunk, he climbs in.)* And
I think I've got the start of a little cold. Did you want
the cigarette?

*(**CARLYLE** stares at him. Then he examines the closed
door and looks again at* **RICHIE***. He considers* **RICHIE***,
and then, thinking he has added it all up, he advances,
almost stalking* **RICHIE***.)*

CARLYLE. You know what I bet? I been lookin' at you real close. It just a way I got about me. And I bet if I was to hang my boy out in front of you, my big boy, man, you'd start wantin' to touch him. Be beggin' and talkin' sweet to ole Carlyle. Am I right or wrong? What do you say?

RICHIE. Pardon?

CARLYLE. You heard me. *(suddenly fearful that he made a mistake, that he misread* **RICHIE***'s actions)* Ohhh. I am so restless, I don't even understand it. *(infuriated by his own confusion)* My big black boy is what I was talkin' about. My thing, man; my rope, Jim. HEY, Richie! *(He lunges close.)* How long you been a punk? Can you hear me? Am I clear? Do I talk funny? *(leaning even closer)* Can you smell the gin on my mouth?

RICHIE. I mean, if you really came looking for Roger, he and Billy are gone to the gymnasium. They were –

CARLYLE. No. I got no athletic abilities. I got none. No moves. I don't know. HEY, Richie! I just got this question I asked. I got no answer.

RICHIE. I don't know – what – you mean.

CARLYLE. I heard me. I understood me. "How long you been a punk?" is the question I asked. Have you got a reply?

RICHIE. Not to that question.

CARLYLE. Who do if you don't? I don't. How'm I gonna?

(Suddenly there is a whistling nearby. **RICHIE** *leaps to his feet and scurries away from the bed. Coming along the walkway, and visible in the windows along the back wall, a soldier passes.)*

CARLYLE. Man, don't you wanna talk to me? Don't you wanna talk to ole Carlyle?

RICHIE. Not at the moment.

CARLYLE. *(Feeling deceived, maybe even deliberately tricked, he moves to* **RICHIE** *who stands nervously near his locker.)* I want to talk to you, man; why don't you want to talk to me? We can be friends. Talkin' back and forth, sharin' thoughts and bein' happy.

RICHIE. I don't think that's what you want.

CARLYLE. What do I want?

RICHIE. I mean, to talk to me.

CARLYLE. What am I doin'? I am talkin'. DON'T YOU TELL ME I AIN'T TALKIN' WHEN I AM TALKIN'! COURSE I AM. Bendin' over backwards. *(Suddenly doubting everything, even if he is actually talking, he is enraged about every humiliation he faces.)* Do you know they still got me in that goddamn P Company? That goddamn transient company. It like they think I ain't got no notion a what a home is. No nose for no home – like I ain't never had no home. I had a home. IT LIKE THEY THINK THERE AIN'T NO PLACE FOR ME IN THIS MOTHER ARMY BUT K.P. ALL SUDSY AND WRINKLED AND SWEATIN'. EVERY DAY SINCE I GOT TO THIS SHIT HOUSE, MISTER! HOW MANY TIMES YOU BEEN ON K.P.? WHEN'S THE LAST TIME YOU PULLED K.P.?

RICHIE. I'm E.D.

CARLYLE. You E.D.? You E.D.? *(another mystery until he thinks he understands)* You Edie, are you? I didn't ask you what you friends call you, I asked when's the last time you had K.P.?

RICHIE. E.D. is "Exempt from Duty." *(gliding away toward his bunk)*

CARLYLE. You ain't got no duties? *(He finds this preposterous.)* What shit you talkin' about? Everybody in this fuckin' army got duties. That what the fuckin' army all about. You ain't got no duties, who got 'em?

RICHIE. Because of my job, Carlyle. I have a very special job. And my friends don't call me Edie. *(He smiles.)* They call me Irene.

CARLYLE. *(desperately trying to figure it all out)* That mean what you sayin' is you kiss ass for somebody, don't it? Good for you. *(pacing near where he lay drunk on the floor)* You know the other night I was sleepin' there. You know.

RICHIE. Yes. *(Lighting a cigarette, he sits near the foot of his bunk.)*

CARLYLE. You remember that? How come you remember that? You sweet.

RICHIE. We don't have people sleeping on our floor that often, Carlyle.

CARLYLE. But the way you crawl over in the night, gimme a big kiss on my joint. That nice.

RICHIE. *(Shocked, he blinks.)* What?

CARLYLE. Or did I dream that? *(Did he? He's really wondering)*

RICHIE. *(laughing in spite of himself)* My God, you're outrageous!

CARLYLE. Maybe you dreamed it. *(That could have happened.)*

RICHIE. What – ? No. I don't know.

CARLYLE. Maybe you did it, then; you didn't dream it.

RICHIE How come you talk so much?

CARLYLE. I don't talk, man, who's gonna talk? YOU? *(circling to the head of* **RICHIE***'s bunk where he perches)* That bore me to death. I don't like nobody's voice but my own. I am so pretty. Don't like nobody else face. *(then viciously right at* **RICHIE***)* You goddamn face ugly fuckin' queer punk!

RICHIE. *(jumping up)* What's the matter with you?

CARLYLE. You goddamn ugly punk face. YOU UGLY!

RICHIE. Nice mouth.

(**RICHIE** *strides to his locker, throwing the book inside.*)

CARLYLE. That's right. That's right. And you got a weird mouth. Like to suck joints.

(*Grabbing a towel,* **RICHIE** *marches toward the door.*)

CARLYLE. Hey, you gonna jus' walk out on me? Where you goin'? You c'mon back. Hear?

RICHIE. That's my bed, for chrissake.

(*He lunges into the hall.*)

CARLYLE. You'd best.

(**CARLYLE** *settles into* **RICHIE***'s bunk, making himself comfortable.*)

CARLYLE. *(taking a pint bottle from his back pocket)* You come back, Richie, I tell you a good joke. Make you laugh, make you cry. *(He takes a big drink.)* That's right. Ole Frank and Jesse, they got the stagecoach stopped, all the peoples lined up – Frank say, "All right, peoples, we gonna rape all the men and rob all the women." Jesse say, "Frank, no, no – that ain't it – we gonna-" And this one little man yell real loud, "You shut up, Jesse; Frank knows what he's doin'." *(laughing, enjoying his joke)*

(BILLY enters. Startled at the sight of CARLYLE on RICH-IE's bunk, BILLY falters, as CARLYLE gestures toward him.)

CARLYLE. Hey, man – ! Hey, you know, they send me over to that Vietnam, I be cool, 'cause I been dodgin' bullets and shit since I been old enough to get on pussy make it happy to know me. I can get on, I can do my job.

(This is the last thing BILLY needs. He still wears his sweat clothes, and looking weary, he crosses to his bunk. CARLYLE studies him, then gazes at the ceiling.)

Yeh. I was just layin' here thinkin' that and you come in and out it come, words to say my feelin'. That my problem. That the black man's problem altogether. You ever considered that? Too much feelin'. He too close to everything. He is, man; too close to his blood, to his body. It ain't that he don't have no good mind, but he BELIEVE in his body. Is – that Richie the only punk in this room, or is there more?

BILLY. *(seated on the edge of his bunk)* What?

CARLYLE. The punk; is he the only punk?

BILLY. He's all right.

CARLYLE. I ain't askin' about the quality of his talent, but is he the only one, is my question?

BILLY. You get your orders yet?

CARLYLE. Orders for what?

BILLY. To tell you where you work.

CARLYLE. I'm P Company, man. I work in P Company. I do K.P. That all. Don't deserve no more. Do you know I been in this army three months and ten days and everybody still doin' the same shit and sayin the same shit and wearin' the same green shitty clothes? I ain't been happy one day, and that a lotta goddamn misery back to back in this ole boy. Is that Richie a good punk? Huh? Is he? He takes care of you and Roger – that how come you in this room, the three of you?

BILLY. What?

CARLYLE. You and Roger are hittin' on Richie, right?

BILLY. He's not queer, if that's what you're sayin'. A little effeminate, maybe, but that's all, no more; if that's what you're sayin'.

CARLYLE. I'd like to get some of him myself if he a good punk, is what I'm sayin'. That's what I'm sayin'! You don't got no understandin' how a man can maybe be a little diplomatic about what he's sayin' sorta sideways, do you? Jesus.

BILLY. He don't do that stuff.

CARLYLE. What stuff?

BILLY. Listen, man. I don't feel too good, you don't mind. *(going to his footlocker for aspirin)*

CARLYLE. What stuff? *(rising, moving toward **BILLY**)*

BILLY. What you're thinkin'.

CARLYLE. What – am I thinkin'?

BILLY. You – know.

CARLYLE. Yes, I do. It in my head, that how come I know. But how do you know? I can see your heart, Billy boy, but you cannot see mine. I am unknown. You – are known.

BILLY. You just – talk fast and keep movin', don't you? Don't ever stay still. *(taking the aspirin)*

CARLYLE. Words to say my feelin', Billy boy.

*(**RICHIE** steps into the room. He sees **BILLY** and **CAR-LYLE**, and stops.)*

CARLYLE. *(smiling at* RICHIE*)* There he is. There he be.

*(*RICHIE *moves to his locker to put away the towel.)*

RICHIE. He's one of them who hasn't come down far out of the trees yet, Billy; believe me.

CARLYLE. You got rudeness in your voice, Richie – you got meanness I can hear about ole Carlyle. You tellin' me I oughta leave – is that what you think you're doin'? You don't want me here?

*(*RICHIE *avoids* CARLYLE, *circling toward* BILLY, *though remaining up near the lockers.)*

RICHIE. You come to see Roger, who isn't here, right? Man like you must have important matters to take care of all over the quad. I can't imagine a man like you not having extremely important things to do all over the world, as a matter of fact, Carlyle.

*(*BILLY *and* RICHIE *are more or less aligned, as they occupy a stage left position and face* CARLYLE.*)*

CARLYLE. *(very apologetic, deferential)* Ohhhh, listen – don't mind all the shit I say. I just talk bad, is all I do; I don't do bad. I got to have friends just like anybody else. I'm just bored and restless, that all; takin' it out on you two. I mean, I know Richie here ain't really no punk, not really. I was just talkin', just jivin' and entertainin' my own self. Don't take me serious, not ever. I get on out and see you all later.

(As CARLYLE *back up toward the door,* RICHIE *moves to the door as if to show* CARLYLE *the way out.)*

CARLYLE. You be cool, hear? Man don't do the jivin', he the one gettin' jived. That what my little brother Henry tell me and tell me.

*(*CARLYLE *backs out and goes and* RICHIE *shuts the door. Silence, as suddenly* RICHIE *and* BILLY *are alone. They meet eyes and then look away.)*

BILLY. I am gonna have to move myself outa here, Roger decides to adopt that sonofabitch.

RICHIE. He's an animal.

BILLY. Yeh, and on top a that, he's a rotten person.

RICHIE. *(laughing)* I think you're probably right.

(**RICHIE** *steps toward* **BILLY,** *but then diverts to his own bunk.* **BILLY** *bends to take off his sneakers, then lies back on his pillow staring, thinking.* **RICHIE** *settles in his own bunk as if to read his book. There is an awkward silence as* **RICHIE** *closes the book and struggles to prepare himself for something.)*

RICHIE. Hey…Billy? *(hesitating)* Billy?

BILLY. Yeh.

RICHIE. You know that story you told the other night?

BILLY. Yeh – ?

RICHIE. You know –

BILLY. What – about it?

RICHIE. Well, was it – about you? *(silence)* I mean, was it – about you? Were you Frankie? *(silence, and wary of even looking at* **BILLY***)* Are – you Frankie? Billy?

(**BILLY** *is slowly sitting up.)*

BILLY. You sonofabitch – !

RICHIE. Or was it really about somebody you knew – ?

BILLY. *(sitting, outraged)* You didn't hear me at all!

RICHIE. I'm just asking a simple question, Billy, that's all I'm doing.

BILLY. You are really sick. You know that? Your brain is really, truly rancid! *(Slipping into his shoes, he starts for the door.)* Do you know there's a theory now it's genetic? That it's all a matter of genes and shit like that?

RICHIE. Everything is not so ungodly cryptic, Billy.

(**BILLY** *veers and confronts* **RICHIE** *who lies in his bunk.)*

BILLY. You. You, man, and the rot it's makin' outa your feeble fuckin' brain.

(**ROGER,** *dressed in civilian clothes, and carrying the basketball bursts in, hurrying straight to his locker.)*

ROGER. Hey, hey, anyone got a couple bucks he can loan me?

BILLY. Rog, where you been?

ROGER. *(throwing his basketball gear into his locker)* I need five. C'mon.

BILLY. Where you been? That asshole friend a yours was here.

ROGER. I know, I know. Can you gimme five?

*(**RICHIE** hurries past **BILLY**, taking money from his billfold.)*

RICHIE. You want five. I got it. You want ten or more, even?

*(**BILLY**, watching **RICHIE** hand the money to **ROGER** turns, and nervously paces around his bunk, where he moves about, worried.)*

BILLY. I mean, we gotta talk about him, man; we gotta talk about him.

ROGER. *(eyeing the money, and putting it into his billfold)* 'Cause we goin' to town together. I jus' run into him out on the quad, man, and he was feelin' real bad 'bout the way he acted, how you guys done him, he was fallin' down apologizin' all over the place.

BILLY. I mean, he's got a lotta weird ideas about us; I'm tellin' you.

ROGER. He's just a little fucked up in his head is all, but he ain't trouble.

(He takes a pork pie hat from his locker along with a pair of sunglasses.)

BILLY. Who needs him? I mean, we don't need him. *(striding away to sit angrily on his footlocker)*

ROGER. *(moving down to face **BILLY**)* You gettin' too nervous, man. Nobody said anything about anybody needin' anybody. I been on the street all my life; he brings back home. I played me a little ball, Billy; took me a shower. I'm feelin' good!

BILLY. I'm tellin' you there's something wrong with him, though.

ROGER. Every black man in the world ain't like me, man; you get used to that idea. You get to know him, and you gonna like him. I'm tellin' you. You get to be laughin' just like me to hear him talk his shit. But you gotta relax.

RICHIE. I agree with Billy, Roger.

ROGER. Well, you guys got it all worked out and that's good, but I am goin' to town with him. Man's got wheels. Got a good head. You got any sense, you'll come with us. *(He steps toward the door.)*

BILLY. What are you talkin' about – come with you? I just tole you he's crazy.

ROGER. And I tole you you're wrong.

RICHIE. We weren't invited.

*(Circling behind **BILLY**, **RICHIE** stands in the aisle between **ROGER** 's and **BILLY** 's bunks)*

ROGER. I'm invitin' you.

RICHIE. No, I don't wanna.

ROGER. *(with a step toward **RICHIE**)* You sure, Richie? C'mon.

RICHIE. No.

ROGER. Billy? He got wheels, we goin' in drinkin', see if gettin' our heads real bad don't just make us feel real good. You know what I mean. I got him right; you got him wrong.

BILLY. But what if I'm right?

ROGER. Billy, Billy, the man is waitin' on me. You know you wanna. Jesus. Bad cat like that gotta know the way. He been to D.C. before. Got cousins here. Got wheels for the weekend.

*(He joins **BILLY** on the footlocker as if on the seat of car, as **RICHIE** sits down behind them on **ROGER** 's bed.)*

ROGER. You always talkin' how you don't do nothin' – you just talk it. Let's do it tonight – stop talkin'. Be cruisin' up and down the strip, leanin' out the window, bad as we wanna be. True cool is a car. We can flip a cigarette out the window – we can watch it bounce. *(putting his hat on* **BILLY***'s head)* Get us some chippies. You know we can. And if we don't he knows a cathouse, it fulla cats.

BILLY. You serious?

RICHIE. You mean you're going to a whorehouse? That's disgusting.

BILLY. Listen who's talkin'. *(looking back, discovering* **RICHIE** *right behind him)* What do you want me to do? Stay here with you?

RICHIE. We could go to a movie or something.

ROGER. I am done with this talkin'. *(taking the hat off* **BILLY***, he stands)* You goin', you stayin'?

BILLY. I don't know.

(Again **BILLY** *looks back at* **RICHIE.***)*

ROGER. Well, I am goin'. *(He puts on the hat.)*

BILLY. I'm going. Okay! I'm going! Going, going, going!

(He runs to his locker.)

RICHIE. Oh, Billy, you'll be scared to death in a cathouse and you know it.

BILLY. BULLSHIT!

(Hastily, putting on a pair civilian trousers. Music is heard from off: The House of the Rising Sun, *sung by The Animals.)*

ROGER. Billy got him a lion tamer 'tween his legs!

(The door bangs open and **CARLYLE** *comes in, dressed now in the same civilian clothes he had when we first saw him, and carring on his shoulder his big transistor radio from which the music plays.)*

CARLYLE. Man, what's going on? I been waitin' like throughout my fuckin' life.

ROGER. Billy's goin', too. He's gotta change.

CARLYLE. He goin', too! Hey! Beautiful! That beautiful!

*(***CARLYLE*** has a big grin, loud happy laugh, as he reaches out for* **BILLY** *to slap his palm in a gesture of welcome.)*

ROGER. Didn't I tell you, Billy?

(**BILLY** *grabs his shirt from his locker and heads for the door.*)

CARLYLE. That beautiful, man; we all goin' to be friends!

RICHIE. What about me, Carlyle?

(**CARLYLE** *looks at* **RICHIE**, *then at* **ROGER**, *and he laughs, as* **ROGER** *grins and they go.* **BILLY**, *the last to leave looks back and meets eyes with* **RICHIE** *who still stands between* **BILLY**'s *and* **ROGER**'s *bunks.* **BILLY** *turns and goes, shutting the door. Then* **CARLYLE**, **ROGER** *and* **BILLY** *move boisterously down the walkway, laughing, the music playing from the radio.* **RICHIE** *watches them, seeing them in one window after the other until they leave the last. Now the music is becoming louder, becoming transition music,* The House of the Rising Sun *over the speakers, as* **RICHIE**, *alone, looks at* **BILLY**'s *bed in front of him, and then he grabs* **BILLY**'s *pillow and pounds the bed over and over, finally tossing the pillow and walking away, as the lights fade to dark and the music builds.*)

Scene Two

(In the dark, The House of the Rising Sun *continues over the speakers and slowly fades as the lights rise,
but the room remains dim. Only the lamp attached to*
RICHIE*'s bunk burns and there is the glow and spill of
the hallway coming through the transom and moonlight
in through the windows.* **BILLY, CARLYLE, ROGER,**
and **RICHIE** *are sprawled about the room.* **BILLY,** *lying
on his stomach, has his head at the foot of his bunk, a
half-empty bottle of beer dangling in his hand. He wears
a blue oxford-cloth shirt and his sneakers lie beside his
bunk.* **ROGER** *is collapsed on his back in his own bunk,
his head also at the foot, a Playboy magazine covering
his face and a half-empty bottle of beer in his hands,
folded on his belly. Having removed his civilian shirt,
he wears a white T-shirt.* **CARLYLE** *is lying on* **RICHIE***'s
bunk, his head at the foot and facing out.* **RICHIE** *is
seated on the floor resting his back against his footlocker.
He is wrapped in a blanket. He drinks from a beer bottle
and beside him stands a second unopened bottle of beer
and a bottle opener.)*

*(They are all dreamy and motionless in the dimness as
the music fades into silence.)*

RICHIE. I don't know where it was, but it wasn't here. And
we were all in it – it felt like – but we all had different
faces. After you guys left, I only dozed for a few minutes, so it couldn't have been long. Roger laughed a
lot and Billy was taller. I don't remember all the details
exactly, and even though we were the ones in it, I
know it was about my father. He was a big man. I was
six. He was a very big man when I was six and he went
away, but I remember him. He started drinking and
staying home making model airplanes and boats and
paintings by the numbers. We had money from mom's
family, so he was just home all the time. And then one
day I was coming home from kindergarten, and as I
was starting up the front steps he came out the door

and he had these suitcases in his hands. He was leaving, see, sneaking out, and I'd caught him. We looked at each other and I just knew and I started crying. He yelled at me, "Don't you cry; don't you start crying." I tried to grab him and he pushed me down in the pavement. And then he was gone. G-O-N-E.

BILLY. *(barely stirring)* And that was it? That was it?

RICHIE. I remember hiding my eyes. I sat on the front steps and hid my eyes and waited.

BILLY. He never came back?

RICHIE. No.

CARLYLE. Ain't that some shit. Now, I'm a jive-time street nigger. I knew where my daddy was all the while. He workin' in this butcher shop two blocks up the street. Ole Mom used to point him out. "There he go. That him – that your daddy." We'd see him on the street, "There he go."

ROGER. Man couldn't see his way to livin' with you – that what you're sayin'?

CARLYLE. Never saw the day.

ROGER. And still couldn't get his ass outta the neighborhood?

*(Having finished the one bottle of beer, **RICHIE** is trying to open the second bottle.)*

CARLYLE. Ain't that a bitch. Poor ole bastard just duck his head – Mom pointin' at him – he git this real goddamn hangdog look like he don't know who we talkin' about and he walk a little faster. Why the hell he never move away I don't know, unless he was crazy. But I don't think so. He come up to me once – I was playin'. "Boy," he says, "I ain't your daddy. I ain't. Your momma's crazy." "Don't you be callin' my momma crazy, Daddy," I tole him. Poor ole thing didn't know what to do.

RICHIE. *(frustrated, giving up, he looks to **BILLY**)* Somebody open this for me? I can't get this open.

CARLYLE. Ole Carlyle get it.

(**CARLYLE** *is quick, reaching to take the bottle.*)

RICHIE. Then there was this once – there was this TV documentary about these bums in San Francisco…

(*Rising,* **RICHIE** *places his empty bottle in the six pack carton on* **BILLY**'s *footlocker, where he then sits down, moving the carton to the floor.*)

…this TV guy was interviewing all these different kinds of bums…and just for maybe ten seconds..,while he was talkin' to this one bum, there was this other one in the background jumpin' around like he thought he was dancin' and wavin' his hat, and even though there wasn't anything about him like my father and I didn't really ever see his face at all, I just kept thinkin': That's him. My dad. He thinks he's dancin'.

(*After a brief silence* **BILLY** *giggles, softly at first, and then a little louder and longer.*)

BILLY. Jesus!

RICHIE. What?

BILLY. That's ridiculous, Richie; sayin' that, thinkin' that. If it didn't look like him, it wasn't him, but you gotta be makin' up a story.

(*Smiling,* **CARLYLE** *approaches* **RICHIE**, *delivering the now opened bottle of beer.*)

CARLYLE. Richie first saw me, he didn't like me much nohow, but he thought it over now, he changed his way a thinkin'. I can see that clear. (*gliding back settles on the floor alongside* **RICHIE**'s *bunk*) We gonna be one big happy family.

RICHIE. (*irritated at* **BILLY** *for laughing at him*) Carlyle likes me, Billy; he thinks I'm pretty.

CARLYLE. (*sitting up a to make his point*) No, I don't think you pretty. A broad is pretty. Punks ain't pretty. Punk – if he good-lookin' – is cute. You cute.

RICHIE. He's gonna steal me right away, little Billy. (*still on* **BILLY**'s *footlocker*) You're so slow, Bill. I prefer a man who's decisive.

BILLY. You just keep at it, you're gonna have us all believin' you are just what you say you are.

RICHIE. Which is more than we can say for you,

BILLY. Jive, jive.

RICHIE. You're arrogant, Billy. So arrogant.

BILLY. What are you – on the rag?

RICHIE. Wouldn't it just bang your little balls if I were!

ROGER. *(rising on his elbow, he faces* **RICHIE***)* Hey, man. What's with you?

RICHIE. Stupidity offends me; lies and ignorance offend me.

BILLY. You know where we was? The three of us? All three of us, earlier on? To the wrong side of the tracks, Richard. One good black upside-down whorehouse where you get what you buy, no jive along with it – so if it's a lay you want and need, you go! Or don't they have faggot whorehouses?

ROGER. *(infuriated)* IF YOU GUYS DON'T CUT THIS SHIT OUT I'M GONNA BUST SOMEBODY'S HEAD!

(Angrily, **ROGER** *flops back on his bunk. There is a silence.* **RICHIE** *rises, moves back to sit on his own footlocker.)*

RICHIE. *(softly, bitterly)* "Where we was," he says. Listen to him. "Where we was." And he's got more school, Carlyle, than you have fingers and – toes.

*(***RICHIE** *slides his foot along the floor until it approaches* **CARLYLE***'s foot.)*

It's this pseudo-earthy quality he feigns – but inside he's all cashmere. *(as his foot touches* **CARLYLE***'s)*

BILLY. That's a lie. *(giggling, looking to* **ROGER***)* I'm polyester, worsted and mohair.

RICHIE. You have a lot of school, Billy; don't say you don't.

BILLY. You said "fingers and toes"; you didn't say "a lot."

CARLYLE. I think people get dumber the more they put their butts into some schoolhouse door.

BILLY. It depends on what the hell you're talkin' about.

(Now BILLY looks in the direction of CARLYLE and RICHIE, and he sees their feet touching.)

CARLYLE. I seen cats back on the block, they knew what was shakin' – then they got into all this school jive and, man, every year they went, they come back they didn't know nothin'.

(BILLY is staring at RICHIE's foot pressed against and rubbing CARLYLE's foot. RICHIE sees BILLY looking. The moment, the silence goes on and on.)

RICHIE. Billy, why don't you and Roger go for a walk?

BILLY. What? *(rising to his knees on the bunk, staring in disbelief)*

RICHIE. Roger asked you to go downtown, you went, you had fun.

ROGER. *(looking, knowing almost instantly what is going on)* I asked you, too.

RICHIE. You asked me; you BEGGED Billy. I said no. Billy said no. You took my ten dollars. You begged Billy. I'm asking you a favor now – go for a walk. Let Carlyle and me have some time.

(Silence. And then CARLYLE sits up, uneasy, wary.)

CARLYLE. That how you work it?

ROGER. Work what?

CARLYLE. Whosever turn it be.

BILLY. No, no, that ain't the way we work it, because we don't work it.

CARLYLE. See? See? There it is – that goddamn education showin' through. All them years in school. Man, didn't we have a good time tonight? You rode in my car. I showed you a good cathouse, all that sweet black pussy. Ain't we friends? Richie likes me. How come you don't like me?

BILLY. 'Cause if you really are doin' what I think you're doin' you're a fuckin' animal!

(**CARLYLE** *leaps to his feet, hand snaking to his pocket, as he strides toward* **BILLY,** *who stands up.*)

ROGER. Billy, no.

(*He jumps between* **CARLYLE** *and* **BILLY.**)

BILLY. NO, WHAT?!

ROGER. Relax, man; no need. *(turning to* **CARLYLE,** *carefully, explaining)* Man, I tole you it ain't goin' on here. We both tole you it ain't goin' on here.

CARLYLE. Don't you jive me, nigger. You goin' for a walk like I'm askin', or not? I wanna get this clear.

ROGER. Man, we live here.

RICHIE. *(bounding to his feet)* It's my house, too, Roger; I live here, too.

ROGER. Don't I know that? Did I say somethin' to make you think I didn't know that?

RICHIE. Carlyle is my guest.

(**RICHIE** *hurries to his bunk, taking off his trousers as he arrives.*)

ROGER. *(whirling, he walks to his bunk)* Fine. He your friend. This is your home. So that mean he can stay. *(He drops into his bed, pulling up the covers.)* It don't mean I gotta leave. I'll catch you all in the mornin'.

BILLY. Roger, what the hell are you doin'?

ROGER. What you better do, Billy. It's gettin' late. I'm goin' to sleep.

BILLY. What? *(bewildered, looking down at* **ROGER**)

ROGER. Go to fucking bed, Billy. Get in your rack, turn your back, and look at the wall.

(*This seems an order, and* **BILLY** *starts to obey.*)

BILLY. You gotta be kiddin'.

ROGER. DO IT!

BILLY. Man – ! *(climbing into his bed)*

ROGER. Yeah – !

BILLY. You mean just –

ROGER. It been goin' on a long damn time, man. You ain't gonna put no stop to it.

(Sudden silence as both **BILLY** *and* **ROGER** *are in their bunks and under the covers with their backs to* **RICHIE** *and* **CARLYLE**. **CARLYLE** *stares at them in disbelief.)*

CARLYLE. You – ain't – serious.

RICHIE. Well, I don't believe it. Of all the childish – infantile – .

CARLYLE. Hey! *(waiting, as if expecting them to do something or explain something)* HEY! Even I got to say this is a little weird, but if this the way you do it – *(turning to* **RICHIE** *by the bed)* – it the way I do it. I don't know.

RICHIE. With them right there? Are you kidding? My God, Carlyle, that'd be obscene. *(pulling away from* **CARLYLE***)*

CARLYLE. Ohhh, man – they backs turned.

RICHIE. No.

CARLYLE. What I'm gonna do?

(Silence. He looks from **RICHIE** *to* **BILLY** *and* **ROGER**, *then back and forth between all of them. He strides toward* **BILLY** *and* **ROGER***.)*

CARLYLE. Don't you got no feelin' for how a man feel? I don't understand you two boys. Unless'n you pair a of motherfuckers. That what you are, you a pair of motherfuckers? You slits, man. DON'T YOU HEAR ME!? I DON'T UNDERSTAND THIS SITUATION HERE. I THOUGHT WE MADE A DEAL!

*(***RICHIE** *picks up his trousers, starts to put them back on but* **CARLYLE**, *incensed, feeling tricked by them all, grabs him.)*

CARLYLE. YOU GET ON YOUR KNEES, YOU PUNK, I MEAN NOW, AND YOU GONNA BE ON MY JOINT FAST OR YOU GONNA BE ONE BUSTED PUNK. AM I UNDERSTOOD?

(He pushes **RICHIE** *to the floor.)*

BILLY. I ain't gonna have this going on here; Roger, I can't.

ROGER. I been turnin' my back on one thing or another all my life.

RICHIE. Jealous, Billy?

BILLY. *(leaping up, striding to the door)* Just go out that door, the two of you. *(pulling the door open)* Go. Go on out in the bushes or out in some field. See if I follow you. See if I care. I'll be right here and I'll be sleepin', but it ain't gonna be done in my house. *(He strides back to his bunk.)* I don't have much in this goddamn army, but HERE is mine.

CARLYLE. I WANT MY FUCKIN' NUT! HOW COME YOU SO UPTIGHT? HE WANTS ME! THIS BOY HERE WANTS ME! WHO YOU TO STOP IT?

ROGER. *(sitting up)* THAT'S RIGHT, Billy. Richie one a those people want to get fucked by niggers, man. It what he know was gonna happen all his life – can be his dream come true. Ain't that right, Richie!

(Jumping to his feet, RICHIE grabs his trousers and puts them on.)

ROGER. Want to make it real in the world, how a nigger is an animal. Give 'em an inch, gonna take a mile. Ain't you some kinda fool Richie? Hear me, Carlyle.

CARLYLE. Man, don't make me no never mind what he think he's provin' an' shit, long as I get my nut. I KNOW I ain't no animal, don't have to prove it.

(Pulling at CARLYLE's arm, RICHIE tries to start him toward the door.)

RICHIE. Let's go. Let's go outside. The hell with it.

CARLYLE. *(tearing himself free, feeling tricked)* Bull shit, Bullshit! I ain't going' no-fuckin'-where-this jive ass ain't runnin' me. Is this your house or not?

ROGER. *(bounding out of bed)* I'm goin' to the fuckin' john, Billy. Hang it up, man; let 'em be.

BILLY. No.

ROGER. I'm smarter than you – do like I'm sayin'.

(**ROGER** *crosses to the door.*)

BILLY. It ain't right.

ROGER. Who gives a big rat's ass!

CARLYLE. Right on, bro! That boy know; he do. Hear him. Look into his eyes.

BILLY. This fuckin' army takin' everything else away from me, they ain't takin' more than they got. I see what I see – I don't run, don't hide.

ROGER. You fuckin' well better learn.

(*He goes, closing the door behind him.*)

CARLYLE. That right. Time for more schoolin'. Lesson number one.

(*Turning out the only light, the lamp clamped to **RICHIE**'s bunk. **CARLYLE** sits on **RICHIE**'s bunk, as they are all shadows in the darkness.*)

You don't see what you see so well in the dark. It dark in the night. Black man got a black body – he disappear.

RICHIE. Not to the hands; not to the fingers. (*moving toward **CARLYLE***)

CARLYLE. You do like you talk, boy, you gonna make me happy.

(*As **BILLY**, nervously watches, then suddenly he bolts toward the door.*)

BILLY. Who says the lights go out? Nobody goddamn asked me if the lights go out.

(**BILLY** *hits the wall switch by the door and the overhead lights flash on, flooding the room with light.*)

CARLYLE. I DO, MOTHERFUCKER, I SAY!

(**CARLYLE** *leaps at **BILLY**, who retreats fearfully as **CARLYLE** advances, driving him back toward the middle window.*)

CARLYLE. I SAY! CAN'T YOU LET PEOPLE BE!?

(As CARLYLE starts back toward RICHIE at his bunk, BILLY grabs up a sneaker from the chair by the lockers and crazily hurls it at CARLYLE, striking him in the back.)

CARLYLE. Goddamn you, boy! *(His hand, snaking into his pocket, comes out with a switchblade.)* I'm gonna cut your ass, just to show you how it feel – and cuttin' can happen. This knife true.

(CARLYLE charges at BILLY, who retreats, his eyes locked on the knife.)

RICHIE. Carlyle, no c'mon.

CARLYLE. Shut up, pussy.

(As BILLY tries to go down the lane between his and ROGER's bunks, he stumbles, walking backwards and sprawls backwards onto ROGER's bed.)

RICHIE. Don't hurt him, for chrissake.

CARLYLE. *(towering over BILLY)* Goddamn man throw a shoe at me, he don't walk around clean in the world thikin' he can throw another. He get some shit come back at him.

(Staring up, BILLY doesn't know which way to go, and when he attempts to rise and run, CARLYLE is instantly in his way, the knife before him.)

CARLYLE. No, no; no, no. Put you hand out there. Put it out.

(BILLY refuses, eyes darting.)

CARLYLE. DO THE THING I'M TELLIN' YOU!

(BILLY's hand rises, almost on its own, and CARLYLE grabs it, holds it.)

CARLYLE. That's it. That's good. See? See?

(Holding BILLY's palm open, CARLYLE drives the knife across the flesh in a slash, and BILLY winces, recoils as the blood flows.)

BILLY. Motherfucker.

RICHIE. Oh, my God, what are you –

(As **CARLYLE** *releases* **BILLY,** *he sits up, holding his wounded hand, crouching over it.* **CARLYLE** *sits down on Roger's bed opposite* **BILLY,** *and lectures* **BILLY,** *as if explaining a lesson.)*

CARLYLE. That you blood. The blood inside you, you don't ever see it there. Take a look how easy it come out – and enough of it come out, you in the middle of the worst goddamn trouble you ever gonna see. And know I'm the man can deal that kinda trouble, easy as I smile. And I smile…easy. Yeah.

*(***BILLY,*** sensing a kind of permission, bolts away, moving up to his wall locker, where he takes out a towel and wraps his hand.* **RICHIE** *stares in shock at both of them, as* **CARLYLE** *strangely depressed, forlornly stands, hoping to explain himself.)*

CARLYLE. Bastard ruin my mood, Richie. He ruin my mood. Fightin' and lovin' real different in the feelin's I got. I see blood come outa somebody like that, it don't make me feel good – hurt me – hurt on somebody I thought was my friend. But I ain't supposed to see. One dumb nigger. No mind, he thinks, no heart, no feelings a gentleness. *(approaching* **RICHIE,** *who recoils)* You see how that ain't true, Richie. *(now he moves toward* **BILLY)** Goddamn man threw a shoe at me. A lotta people woulda cut his heart out. *(wandering, rambling to explain, he ends up near the middle window and chair)* I gotta make him know he throw shit, he get shit. But I don't hurt him bad. I don't hurt him bad, you see what I mean?

*(***BILLY*** *'s back is to them, and he turns now, he gestures revealing that he holds his straight edge razor in one hand, a bloody towel wrapped around the other.* **CARLYLE** *tenses, fixing on the razor.)*

BILLY. Jesus…H…Christ…! Do you know what I'm doin'? Do you know what I'm standin' here doin'? *(in disbelief and growing relief)* I'm a twenty-four-year-old goddamn college graduate – intellectual goddamn scholar type

– and I got a razor in my hand. I'm thinkin' about comin' up behind one black human being and I'm thinkin' nigger this and nigger that – I wanna cut his throat.

(With his relief becoming joy, he discards the razor, tossing it clattering into the nearby trash can.)

BILLY. That is ridiculous. I never faced anybody in my life with anything to kill them. You understand me? I don't have a thing on the line here!

(The door opens and **ROGER** *steps in.* **CARLYLE,** *guiltily drops into the chair stationed there at the window between the lockers, hiding the knife from* **ROGER,** *as* **BILLY** *goes to* **ROGER.** *)*

BILLY. Look at me, Roger, look at me. I got a cut palm – I don't know what happened.

ROGER. *(looking at* **BILLY** *'s hand)* Damn! *(taking hold of* **BILLY,** *leading him to his footlocker)*

BILLY. Jesus Christ, I got sweat all over me when I think a what I was near to doin'. I swear it. *(sitting on his own footlocker)* I mean, do I think I need a reputation as a killer, a bad man with a knife? Bullshit! I need shit!

*(***ROGER** *is attempting to treat* **BILLY** *'s hand with gauze and peroxide taken from his own footlocker.)*

I got sweat all over me. I got the mile record in my hometown. I did a four fourty-two in high school, and that's the goddamn record in Windsor County. *(pulling free, almost joyous as he addresses* **CARLYLE** *and* **RICHIE** *)* I don't need approval from either one of the pair of you.

(Advancing on **RICHIE,** *who, near his bunk, turns away.)*

You wanna be a goddamn swish – a goddamn faggot-queer – Go! Suckin' cocks and takin' it in the ass, the thing of which you dream – Go! And you –

(stepping toward **CARLYLE,** *who still sits on the chair)*

You wanna be a bad-assed animal, man, get it on – go – but I wash my hands, I am not human as you are. I put you down – *(strangely giddy, almost happy, veering back at* RICHIE*)* I put you down – you gay little piece of shit cake – shit cake!

(Spinning and finding CARLYLE *on his feet, he walks toward his locker and so toward* CARLYLE, *but he is done with them both, free of them both.)*

And you – you are your own goddamn fault, Sambo! Sambo! *(laughing)* Sambo!

ROGER. *(Fed up, he slams his hand on his locker.)* Damnit, Billy!

*(*BILLY *and* CARLYLE *are like strangers passing on a street who bump into each other.)*

BILLY. Ahhhhhhhh. *(pushing at* CARLYLE*)*

RICHIE. *(turning to see)* Well fuck you, Billy.

(In the confusion, in the seemingly accidental collision, CARLYLE *has stabbed* BILLY, *who now pushes at* CAR-LYLE.*)*

BILLY. Get away, get away.

(As CARLYLE *pulls free,* BILLY *goes walking on toward his locker, as if on an ordinary errand, his hands holding his belly.)*

RICHIE. You're sooo messed up.

*(*ROGER, *angry at* BILLY *for the word "Sambo.")*

ROGER. Man, what's the matter with you?

CARLYLE. *(thinking* ROGER *is speaking to him)* Don't nobody talk that weird shit to me, you understand?

ROGER. *(turning to* CARLYLE*)* You jive, man. That's all you do – jive!

*(*BILLY, *striding swiftly, walks flat into the wall lockers. He bounces, stands there, leaning against them.)*

RICHIE. Billy! Oh, Billy!

BILLY. Ahhhhhhhh. Ahhhhhhhh.

(ROGER *looks at* CARLYLE *and back to* BILLY, *who turns from the lockers, starts to walk again, now staggering and moving toward them.*)

RICHIE. *(hushed)* I think…he stabbed him. I think Carlyle stabbed Billy. Roger!

(ROGER *hastens to* BILLY, *who is staggering downstage and angled away, hands clenched over his belly. They all see his hands, a hint of blood.*)

BILLY. Shut up! It's just a cut, it's just a cut. He cut my hand, he cut my gut.

(Collapsing to his knees at the side of his footlocker, he struggles to conceal the wound and remain calm.)

It took the wind out of me, scared me, that's all.

ROGER. Man, are you all right?

(No one is sure what happened. RICHIE *thinks* BILLY *has been stabbed, while* BILLY *pretends he isn't hurt. Now, as* ROGER *approaches* BILLY, *who turns away to hide the wound,* RICHIE *sees blood. They all see blood, and all begin talking and yelling simultaneously.*)

CARLYLE. *(overlap)* You know what I was learnin', he was learnin' to talk all that weird shit, cuttin', baby, cuttin', the ways and means a shit, man, razors –

RICHIE. *(overlap)* – Carlyle, you stabbed him; you stabbed him –

ROGER. *(overlap)* – You all right? Or what? He slit you or –

BILLY. *(overlap)* – Just took the wind outta me, scared me –

CARLYLE. – Ohhh, pussy, pussy, pussy. Carlyle know what he do.

ROGER. *(trying to help* BILLY *up)* Get up, okay? Get up on the bed.

BILLY. I am on the bed.

ROGER. What?

RICHIE. No, Billy, no you're not.

BILLY. *(weakly)* Shut up….

RICHIE. *(trying to help him, calm him)* You're on the floor.

BILLY. *(emphatically)* I'm on the bed. I'm on the bed. *(but he looks at his knees on the floor)* What?!

ROGER. Let me see what he did. *(trying to move **BILLY**'s hands clenched on the wound)* Let me see where he got you.

BILLY. Nooooo.

ROGER. *(leaping toward **CARLYLE**)* What did you do?

CARLYLE. *(hunching his shoulders, ducking)* Shut up.

ROGER. What did you do, nigger – you slit him or stick him? *(turning back to **BILLY**)* Billy, let me see.

BILLY. *(doubling over till his head hits the floor.)* Noooooo! Shit, shit, shit.

RICHIE. *(suddenly sobbing, bouncing on his knees on the bunk)* Oh, my God, my God, ohhhh, ohhhh, ohhhh.

CARLYLE. FUCK IT, FUCK IT, I STUCK HIM. I TURNED IT. This mother army break my heart. I can't be out there where it pretty, don't wanna live! Wash me clean, shit face!

RICHIE. Ohhhh, ohhhh, ohhhhhhhhhhh. Carlyle stabbed Billy, oh, ohhhh, I never saw such a thing in my life. Ohhhhh.

*(As **ROGER** is trying to gently, fearfully, straighten **BILLY** up.)*

RICHIE. Don't die, Billy; don't die.

ROGER. Shut up and go find somebody to help. Richie, GO!

RICHIE. Who? I'll go, I'll go. *(jumping off the bunk)*

ROGER. I don't know. JESUS CHRIST! DO IT!

RICHIE. *(backing for the door)* Okay. Okay. Billy, don't die. Don't die. *(He turns and runs.)*

ROGER. The sarge, or C.Q!

*(**ROGER** is watching **RICHIE** run out the door when suddenly **BILLY** doubles over, vomiting blood.)*

BILLY. Ohhhhhhhhh. Blood. Blood.

ROGER. Be still, be still.

BILLY. *(pulling at the nearby blanket **RICHIE** discarded earlier)* I want to stand up. I'm – vomiting – blood. What does that mean?

ROGER. I don't know.

BILLY. Yes, yes, I want to stand up. Give me blanket, blanket. *(rolling back and forth, struggling to get the blanket over him.)*

ROGER. RIICCHHHIIIEEEEEE!

(as BILLY is furiously grappling with the blanket)

No, no. Go easy.

(ROGER looks at CARLYLE, who is slumped over on the chair, muttering to himself. ROGER looks to the door, then back to BILLY.)

ROGER. Wait on, be tight, be cool.

(He runs for the door to get help.)

BILLY. Cover me. Cover me.

(BILLY finally gets the blanket over his face. For a moment, he grows still, as he lies there beneath his blanket. Silence. And then CARLYLE senses the quiet; he turns, looks. Slowly, he rises and walks to where BILLY lies. He stands over him, the knife hanging loosely from his left hand as he reaches with his right to gently take the blanket and lift it slowly from BILLY's face, trying to see how much trouble he's in. They look at each other. BILLY reaches up and touches CARLYLE's hand holding the blanket.)

BILLY. I don't want to talk to you right now, Carlyle. All right? Where's Roger? Do you know where he is? Don't stab me anymore, Carlyle, okay? I was wrong doin' what I did. I know that now. Carlyle, promise me you won't stab me anymore. I couldn't take it. Okay? I'm cold...my blood...is...

(From the hallway beyond the door comes ROONEY's voice.)

ROONEY. *(offstage)* Cokesy? Cokesy wokesy?

(ROONEY staggers into the room, very drunk, a beer bottle in his hand.)

ROONEY. Ollie-ollie oxen-freeee.

(CARLYLE *drops the blanket back over* BILLY *and retreats, quickly. He would flee but* ROONEY *is between him and the door.*)

ROONEY. How you all doin'? *(seeing* BILLY *lying covered on t the floor)* Everybody drunk, huh? I los' my friend.

(CARLYLE *has gone as far away as he can in the room, standing with his back to* ROONEY, *who studies him.*)

ROONEY. Who are you, soldier?

(CARLYLE *turns slowly, downcast and searching for a route past* ROONEY.*)*

ROONEY. Who are you, soldier?

(RICHIE *dashes into the room. He looks at* ROONEY *and* CARLYLE *and cannot understand what is going on.*)

RICHIE. Ohhhhhh, Sergeant Rooney, I've been looking for you everywhere – where have you been? Carlyle stabbed Billy, he stabbed him.

ROONEY. What?

RICHIE. Carlyle stabbed Billy.

ROONEY. Who's Carlyle?

RICHIE. *(pointing)* He's Carlyle.

(CARLYLE *advances, seeking a way out of the room.*)

RICHIE. *(hovering in the doorway)* Carlyle, don't hurt anybody more!

ROONEY. You got a knife there? What's with the knife? What's going on here?

(As CARLYLE *hides the knife along his thigh,* ROONEY *is suddenly alert, the beer bottle in his hand as a weapon, as he adjusts to keep* CARLYLE *from the door.*)

ROONEY. Wait! Now wait!

RICHIE. Carlyle, don't!

(RICHIE *runs from the room.*)

ROONEY. You watch your step, you understand. You see what I got here?

(Waving his beer bottle, threateningly, **ROONEY** *watches* **CARLYLE**, *on the opposite side of* **ROGER**'s *bunk, prowling upstage as if he hopes to flee along the lockers, but* **ROONEY** *counters, blocking the way.)*

ROONEY. You watch your step, motherfucker. Relax. I mean, we can straighten all this out. We –

(**CARLYLE** *feints as if to lunge, and* **ROONEY** *tenses.)*

I'm just askin' what's goin' on, that's all I'm doin'. No need to get all –

(**CARLYLE** *feints again, then swipes at the air again.)*

Motherfucker. Motherfucker. *(Tensing, his body gathering itself for some mighty effort he gives the eagle yell.)* Eeeeeeeee-aaaaaaaaahhhhhhhh! Eeeeeeeeaaaaaaaaaahhhhhhhh!

(**CARLYLE** *is startled, looking left and right for a way to go.)*

ROONEY. Goddamnit, I'll cut you good. *(swinging and breaking the bottle on the edge of the lockers, he drops the remnants, grabbing his hand)* Ohhhhhh! Ohhhhhhhhhhhhhhh!

(**CARLYLE** *bolts, finding a pathway out of the room. Holding his cut hand,* **ROONEY** *steps after* **CARLYLE**, *but then stops and looks around.)*

ROONEY. I hurt myself. *(seeing a sock on* **BILLY**'s *bed, he heads for it)* I cut myself. *(wrapping the hand in the sock)* I hurt my hand like some stupid idiot. Just cut –

(Hearing a noise behind him, he whirls and sees **CAR-LYLE***)*

ROONEY. I hurt my hand, goddamnit!

(But **CARLYLE** *is upon him before he has even fully turned, the knife plunging into* **ROONEY**'s *belly.)*

ROONEY. I hurt my hand! What are you doing? What are you doing? WAIT! WAIT! *(flailing, turning away, going to his knees, as the knife drives into him again)* No fair. No fair!

(**ROGER** *runs into the room, skidding to a stop, as headed for* **BILLY**, *he is met by* **CARLYLE** *on* **ROONEY**. **ROGER** *grabs* **CARLYLE**, *pulling him off of* **ROONEY**.*

CARLYLE *leaps free, sending* ROGER *flying backward.* ROONEY *is crawling as if to hide under* BILLY's *bunk, where he stops.* CARLYLE *approaches* ROGER, *whimpering, stroking the blood on his shirt as if to wipe it away.* ROGER *backs away as* CARLYLE *waves the knife at him.)*

CARLYLE. You don't tell nobody on me you saw me do this, I let you go, okay? Ohhhhhhh. *(rubbing, rubbing at the shirt)* Ohhhh, how'm I gonna get back to the world now, I got all this mess to –

ROGER. What happened? That you – I don't understand that you did this! That you did –

CARLYLE. YOU SHUT UP! Don't be talkin' all that weird shit to me – don't you go talkin' all that weird shit!

ROGER. Noo!

CARLYLE. I'm Carlyle, man. You know me. You know me.

(CARLYLE *runs out the door, and* ROGER, *alone, looks about at the mayhem,* BILLY *on the floor,* ROONEY *under the bunk, the broken bottle. He moves toward* BILLY, *who is shifting, undulating on his back.)*

BILLY. Carlyle, no; oh, Christ, don't stab me anymore. I'll die. I will – I'll die. Don't make me die. I'll get my dog after you. I'LL GET MY DOG AFTER YOU!

(ROGER *is saying, "Oh, Billy, man, Billy." He is trying to hold* BILLY, *applying pressure with his hand and some kind of cloth to the wound. Now he lifts* BILLY *into his arms.)*

ROGER. Oh, Billy; oh, man. GODDAMNIT Billy!

(*An* MP LIEUTENANT. *steps into the room, his .45 automatic drawn, and he levels it at* ROGER.)

LIEUTENANT. Freeze, soldier! Not a quick move out of you. Just real slow, straighten your ass up.

(ROGER *has gone rigid; the* LIEUTENANT *is advancing on him. Tentatively,* ROGER *looks.)*

ROGER. Huh? No.

LIEUTENANT. Get your ass against the lockers.

ROGER. Sir, no. I –

LIEUTENANT. *(hurling* **ROGER** *face first against the wall lockers)* MOVE!

(Another MP, **PFC HINSON,** *comes in, followed by* **RICHIE,** *flushed and breathless.)*

LIEUTENANT. Hinson, cover this bastard.

HINSON. Yes, sir.

*(***HINSON** *draws his .45 automatic, closing on* **ROGER,** *while the* **LIEUTENANT** *frisks* **ROGER,** *who is spread-eagled at the lockers.)*

RICHIE. What? Oh, sir, no, no. Roger, what's going on?

LIEUTENANT. I'll straighten this shit out.

ROGER. Tell 'em to get the gun off me, Richie.

LIEUTENANT. Shut up!

RICHIE. But, sir, sir, he didn't do it. Not him.

LIEUTENANT. *(shoving* **RICHIE** *out of the way)* I told you, all of you, to shut up. *(moving to examine* **ROONEY**'s *body)* Jesus, God, this sergeant is cut to shit. He's cut to shit. *(He hurries to* **BILLY**'s *body.)* This man too. Awful.

(As **CARLYLE** *appears in the doorway, his hands cuffed behind him,* **PFC CLARKE** *pushing him forward.)*

CLARKE. Sir, I got this guy on the street, runnin' like a streak a shit.

(As **CLARKE** *compels the struggling* **CARLYLE** *forward,* **RICHIE** *backs up against the wall locker near where* **ROGER** *still stands spread-eagle, his hands pressed against the metal.)*

RICHIE. *(pointing at* **CARLYLE***)* He did it! Him, him!

CARLYLE. What is going on here? I don't know what is going on here!

CLARKE. He's got blood all over him, sir. All over him.

LIEUTENANT. What about the knife?

CLARKE. No, sir. He must have thrown it away.

(As a **FOURTH MP** *arrives in the doorway, and* **HINSON** *leaves* **ROGER,** *bending to examine* **ROONEY.***)*

LIEUTENANT. You throw it away, soldier?

CARLYLE. Oh, you thinkin' about how my sister got happened, too. Oh, you ain't so smart as you think you are! No way!

LIEUTENANT. What happened here? I want to know what happened here.

HINSON. *(examining* BILLY*'s body, he straightens)* They're both dead, sir. Both of them.

LIEUTENANT. I know they're both dead. That's what I'm talkin' about.

CARLYLE. Chicken blood, sir. Chicken blood and chicken hearts is what all over me. I was goin' on my way, these people jump out the bushes be pourin' it all over me. Chicken blood and chicken hearts. *(thrusting his hands at* CLARKE*)* You goin' take these cuffs off me, boy?

LIEUTENANT. Sit him down, Clarke. Sit him down and shut him up.

(CLARKE grabs CARLYLE, begins to move him.)

CARLYLE. This my house, sir. This my goddamn house.

LIEUTENANT. I said to shut him up.

CLARKE. *(banging his nightstick against the wall)* Move it; move!

(CLARKE pushes CARLYLE down onto the chair by the door. HINSON and the FOURTH MP exit.)

CARLYLE. I want these cuffs taken off my hands.

CLARKE. You better do like you been told. You better sit and shut up!

CARLYLE. I'm gonna be thinkin' over here. I'm gonna be thinkin' it all over. I got plannin' to do. I'm gonna be thinkin' in my quietness; don't' you be makin' no mistake.

(He slumps over, muttering to himself. HINSON and the FOURTH MP return, carrying a stretcher. They cross to BILLY, discussing how to go about the lift. They will lift him and carry him out.)

LIEUTENANT. *(to* RICHIE*)* You're Wilson?

RICHIE. No, sir. *(indicating* BILLY*)* That's Wilson. I'm Douglas.

LIEUTENANT. *(to* ROGER*)* And you're Moore. And you sleep here.

ROGER. Yes, sir.

RICHIE. Yes, sir. And Billy slept here and Sergeant Rooney was our sergeant and Carlyle was a transient, sir. He was a transient from P Company.

LIEUTENANT. *(scrutinizing* ROGER*)* And you had nothing to do with this? *(to* RICHIE*)* He had nothing to do with this?

ROGER. No, sir, I didn't.

RICHIE. No, sir, he didn't. I didn't either. Carlyle went crazy and he got into a fight and it was awful. I didn't even know what it was about exactly.

LIEUTENANT. How'd the sergeant get involved?

RICHIE. Well, he came in, sir.

ROGER. I had to run off to call you, sir. I wasn't here.

RICHIE. Sergeant Rooney just came in – I don't know why – he heard all the yelling, I guess – and Carlyle went after him. Billy was already stabbed.

CARLYLE. *(rising, his wild-eyed manner that of a man taking charge)* All right now, you gotta be gettin' the fuck outa here. All of you. I have decided enough of this shit has been goin' on around here and I am tellin' you to be getting' these motherfuckin' cuffs off me and you be gettin' me a bus ticket home. I am quittin' this jive-time army.

LIEUTENANT. You are doin' what?

CARLYLE. No, I ain't gonna be quiet. No way. I am quittin' this goddamn –

LIEUTENANT. You shut the hell up, soldier. I am ordering you.

CARLYLE. I don't understand you people! Don't you people understand when a man be talkin' English at you to say his mind? I have quit the army!

(HINSON returns.)

LIEUTENANT. Get him outa here!

RICHIE. What's the matter with him?

LIEUTENANT. Hinson! Clarke!

(They move, grabbing CARLYLE, draggin him, struggling, toward the door.)

CARLYLE. Oh, no. Oh, no. You ain't gonna be doin' me no more. I been tellin' you. To get away from me. I am stayin' here. This my place, not your place. You take these cuffs off me like I been tellin' you! *(howling in the hallway by now)* My poor little sister Lin Sue understood what was goin' on here! She tole me! She knew! You better be gettin' these cuffs off me!

(Silence. ROGER, RICHIE, and the LIEUTENANT are all staring at the door. The LIEUTENANT turns, crosses to the foot of ROGER's bunk.)

LIEUTENANT. All right now. I will be getting to the bottom of this. You know I will be getting to the bottom of this. *(taking forms from his pocket)*

RICHIE. Yes, sir.

(HINSON and the FOURTH MP return with another stretcher for ROONEY, who they begin dragging from under the bunk.)

LIEUTENANT. Fill out these forms. *(handing forms to ROGER and RICHIE)* I want your serial number, rank, your MOS, the NCIOC of your work. Any leave coming up will be cancelled. Tomorrow at 0800 you will report to my office at the provost marshal's headquarters. You know where that is?

(With ROONEY on their stretcher, HINSON and the FOURTH MP lift and start to go.)

ROGER. Yes, sir.

RICHIE. Yes, sir.

LIEUTENANT. Be prepared to do some talking. Two perfectly trained and primed strong U.S. Army soldiers got cut to shit up here. We are going to find out how and why. Is that clear?

*(They watch **ROONEY** being carried out the door.)*

RICHIE. Yes, sir.

ROGER. Yes, sir.

*(The **LIEUTENANT** looks at each of them, surveys the room, pivots and goes. **ROGER** and **RICHIE** stand almost side by side in the suddenly, strangely empty room for a breath of silence and then another.)*

RICHIE. Oh, my God. Oh. Oh.

*(**RICHIE** moves slowly, weakly, in a daze to his bunk and sits hunched down. **ROGER** stands, looking, looking and then he walks purposefully to the mops hanging on the wall near the door. He takes one down, grabs the bucket and moves to the spot where **BILLY** lay. He begins mopping up the blood. **RICHIE**, in distress, watches.)*

RICHIE. What…are you doing?

ROGER. This area a mess, man.

RICHIE. That's Billy's blood, Roger. His blood.

ROGER. Is it?

RICHIE. I feel awful.

*(Dragging the bucket, carrying the mop, he moves near **BILLY**'s bunk and the blood **ROONEY** left. He begins to mop.)*

ROGER. How come you made me waste all that time talkin' shit to you, Richie? All my time talkin' shit, and all the time you was a faggot, man; you really was. You shoulda jus' tole ole Roger. He don't care. All you gotta do is tell me.

RICHIE. I've been telling you. I did.

ROGER. Jive, man, jive!

RICHIE. No!

ROGER. You did bullshit all over us! ALL OVER US!

RICHIE. I just wanted to hold his hand, Billy's hand, to talk to him, go to the movies hand in hand like he would with a girl or I would with someone back home.

ROGER. But he didn't wanna! He didn't wanna.

RICHIE. *(sobbing)* He did.

(Finished now, ROGER moves to put the mop and bucket away.)

ROGER. No, man.

RICHIE. He did. He did. It's not my fault.

(ROGER slams the bucket into the corner, rams the mop into the bucket. Furious, he strides to RICHIE.)

ROGER. You know what you oughta do? Get you a little mustache. Get you some hair around yo' mouth. Make it look like what you think it is. You do that!

(Behind ROGER, SERGEANT COKES, appears in the open doorway, grinning and lifting a wine bottle.)

COKES. Hey! Hey! What a day, gen'l'men. How you all doin'?

(RICHIE, in despair, rolls onto his belly. COKES is very, very happy.)

ROGER. *(crossing toward his own bunk)* Hello, Sergeant Cokes.

COKES. *(friendly and casual, following ROGER for a step or two)* How you all doin'? Where's ole Rooney? I lost him

ROGER. What?

COKES. We had a hell of a day, ole Rooney and me, lemme tell you. We been playin' hide-and-go-seek, and I was hidin', and now I think maybe he started hidin' without tellin' me he was gonna and I can't find him and I thought maybe he was hidin' up here.

RICHIE. Sergeant, he –

ROGER. *(pointedly to RICHIE)* No. *(and to COKES)* No, we ain't seen him.

COKES. I gotta find him. He knows how to react in a tough situation. He didn't come up here looking for me?

ROGER. *(moving to tidy up, picking up beer bottles from around his and BILLY's bunks)* We was goin' to sleep, Sarge. Got to get up early. You know the way this mother army is.

COKES. *(Drifting, he hesitates in front of the middle window.)* You don't mind I sit here a little. Wait on him. Got a little wine. You can have some. *(He takes a big drink and then looks out the window.)* We got back into the area – we had been downtown – he wanted to play hide-and-go-seek. I tole him okay, I was ready for that. He hid his eyes. *(Turning to them now, he settles on the chair in front of the middle window.)* So I run and hid in the bushes and then under this Jeep. 'Cause I thought it was better. I hid and I hid and I hid. He never did come. So finally, I got tired – I figured I'd give up, come lookin' for him. I was way over by the movie theater. I don't know how I got there. Anyway, I got back here and I figured maybe he come up here lookin' for me, figurin' I was hidin' up with you guys. You ain't seen him, huh?

ROGER. No, we ain't seen him. I tole you that, Sarge. We ain't seen him. *(cleaning up the beer bottles near **RICHIE**'s bunk)*

COKES. Oh.

RICHIE. Roger!

ROGER. *(a little hushed)* He's drunk, Richie! He's blasted drunk. Got a brain turned to mush!

COKES. *(in deep agreement)* That ain't no lie.

ROGER. Let it be for the night, Richie. Let him be for the night.

COKES. I still know what's goin' on, though. *(advancing on **ROGER** to make sure he understands)* Never no worry about that. I always know what's goin' on. I always know. Don't matter what I drink or how much I drink. I always still know what's goin' on. *(weaving for the door)* But...I'll be going maybe and look for Rooney. *(But as he's about to go out the door, he stops, pivots and comes back.)* But...I mean, we could be doin' that forever. Him and me. Me under the Jeep. He wants to find me, he goes to the Jeep. I'm over here. He comes here. I'm gone. You know, maybe I'll just wait a little while more. I'm here. He'll find me then if he comes here. You guys want another drink? *(wandering to* **BILLY**'s *bed, where he sits facing out, halfway straddling the bed as he takes another guzzle of wine)* Jesus, what a goddamn day we had. Me and Rooney started drivin' and we was comin' to this intersection and out comes this goddamn Chevy. I try to get around her, but no dice. BINGO! I hit her in the left rear. She was furious. I didn't care. I gave her my name and number. My car had a headlight out, the fender bashed in. Rooney wouldn't stop laughin'. I didn't know what to do. So we went to D.C. to this private club I know. Had ten or more snorts and decided to get back here after playin' some snooker. That was fun. On the way, we picked up this kid from the engineering unit, hitchhiking. I'm starting to feel real clearheaded now. So I'm comin' around this corner and all of a sudden there's this car stopped dead in front of me. He's not blinkin' to turn or anything. I slam on the brakes, but it's like puddin' the way I slide into him. There's a big noise and we yell. Rooney starts laughin' like crazy and the kid jumps outa the back and says he's gonna take the fuckin' bus. The guy from the other car is swearin' at me. My car's still workin' fine, so I move it off to the side and tell him to do the same, while we wait for the cops. He says he wants his car right where it is and he had the right of way cause he was makin' a legal turn. So we're waitin' for the cops. Some cars go by. The guy's car is this big fuckin' Buick. Around the corner comes this little red Triumph. The driver's this blond kid got this blond girl next to him. You can see what's gonna happen. There's this fuckin' car sittin' there, nobody in it. So the Triumph goes crashin' into the back of the Buick with nobody in it. BIFF – BANG – BOOM. And everything stops. We're staring. It's all still. And then that fuckin' Buick kinda shudders and starts to move. It starts to roll from the impact. And it rolls just far enough to get where the road starts a downgrade. It's driftin' to the right. It's driftin' to the shoulder and over it and onto this hill, where it's pickin' up speed cause the hill is steep and then it disappears over the side, and into the dark, just rollin' real quiet. Nobody in it. Rooney falls over, he's laughin' so hard. I don't know what to do. In a minute the cops come and in another minute some guy comes runnin' up over the hill to tell us some other guy had got run over by this car with nobody in it. We didn't know what to think. This was fuckin' unbelievable to us. But we found out later, this guy got hit over the head with a bottle in a bar and when he staggered out the door it was just as this fucking Buick came along. And then the car, after hittin' this guy, comes to this uphill place, where the uphill part slows it and stops it and backs it up until it finally stops and sits there. With nobody in it. Rooney is screamin' at me how we been in four goddamn accidents and fights and how we have got out clean. *(He thinks for a second.)* So then we got everything all straightened out and we come back here to play hide-and-seek cause that's what ole Rooney wanted. *(Standing, he starts for the door.)* Only now I can't find him.

(RICHIE, lying on his belly, shudders, and sobs burst out of him, as COKES is passing. COKES, blinking, stops and turns to study RICHIE.)

COKES. What's up? Hey, what're you cryin' about, soldier? Hey?

(RICHIE cannot help himself. COKES turns to ROGER, who sits on his own bed.)

COKES. What's he cryin' about?

ROGER. *(disgustedly)* He's cryin' cause he's a queer.

COKES. Oh. *(nodding, thinking a second)* You a queer, boy?

RICHIE. Yes, Sergeant.

COKES. Oh…How long you been a queer?

ROGER. All his fuckin' life.

RICHIE. I don't know.

COKES. *(to ROGER)* Don't be yellin' mean at him.

(COKES settles down on RICHIE's footlocker, his back more or less to RICHIE.)

COKES. Boy, I tell you it's a real strange thing the way havin' these heart arrhythmias give you a lotta funny thoughts about things. Two months ago – or maybe even yesterday – I'da called a boy who was a queer a lotta awful names. But now I just wanna be figurin' things out. I got these arrhythmias in my heart, and if they was to all come in a bunch, like a horde, that'd be the end of me. Just sittin' here even. Out like a light. I mean, you ain't kiddin' me about ole Rooney, are you, boys, cause of how I'm a sergeant and you're enlisted men, so you got some idea a vengeance on me? You ain't doin' that, are you, boys?

ROGER. No.

RICHIE. Ohhhh. Jesus. Ohhhh. I don't know what's hurtin' in me.

COKES. No, no, boy. You listen to me. You gonna be okay. There's a lotta worse things in this world than bein' a queer. I seen a lot of 'em, too. I mean, you could have a bum heart. That's worse. That can kill you. *(As* **RICHIE** *sobs,* **COKES** *looks back at him.)* I mean, it's okay. You listen to the ole sarge. Maybe if I was you and you was me, I wouldn't have this bullshit going on in my heart. Who's to say? Lived a whole different life. *(standing)* Who's to say? I keep thinkin' there was maybe somethin' I coulda done different. Maybe not drunk so much. Or if I'd killed more gooks, or more krauts or more dinks. I was kinda merciful sometimes. Or if I'd had a wife and I had some kids. Never had any. But my mother did and she died of it anyway. Gives you a whole funny different way a lookin' at things, I'll tell you. Ohhhh, Rooney, Rooney. *(slight pause as his eyes fall upon* **BILLY**'s *footlocker in front of him)* Or if I'd let that little gook outa that spider hole he was in, I was sittin' on it. I'd let him out now, he was in there. *(moving to the footlocker, his gaze fixed upon it)* Oh, how'm I ever gonna forget it? That funny little guy. I'm runnin' along, he pops up outa that hole. I'm never gonna forget him – how'm I ever gonna forget him? I see him and dive, goddamn bullet hits me in the side, I'm midair, everything's turnin' around. I go over the edge of this ditch and I'm crawlin' real fast. I lost my rifle. Can't find it. Then I come up behind him. He's half out of the hole. I bang him on top of his head, stuff him back into the hole with a grenade for company. *(Flipping open the footlocker lid and slamming it down, he sits on it.)* Then I'm sittin' on the lid and it's made out of steel. I can feel him in there, though, bangin' and yellin' under me.., *(He rattles the footlocker lid beneath him.)* ...and his yelling I can hear is beggin for me to let him out. It was like a goddamn Charlie Chaplin movie, everybody fallin' down and clumsy, and him in there yellin' and bangin' away, and I'm just sittin' there lookin' around. And he was Charlie Chaplin. I don't know who I was. And then he blew up.

*(Silence. **ROGER** rises and walks to the door, which he gently closes before switching off the overhead lights. The transom glows, as **ROGER** starts back for his bunk, and **COKES** shifts, as if to get more comfortable.)*

COKES. Maybe I'll just get a little shut-eye right sittin' here while I'm waitin' for ole Rooney. We figure it out. All of it. You don't mind I just doze a little here, you boys?

ROGER. No.

RICHIE. No.

*(**COKES** sits there, leaning back on the footlocker in faint light, fingers entwined, trying to sleep.)*

COKES. I mean, he was like Charlie Chaplin. And then he blew up.

ROGER. *(climbing into bed)* Sergeant... maybe you was Charlie Chaplin, too.

COKES. No. No. *(he thinks)* No. I don't know who I was.

ROGER. You think he was singin' it?

COKES. What?

ROGER. You think he was singin' it?

COKES. Oh, yeah. Oh, yeah; he was singin' it.

(Using a made up, makeshift language of imitation Korean, **COKES** *begins to sing to the tune of "Beautiful Streamer." Perhaps a little bitter at the start, the song becomes a dream, a lullaby, a lament, a farewell.)*

COKES. Yo no som lo no
Ung toe lo knee
Ra so me la lo
La see see oh doe.
Doe no tee ta ta
Too low see see
Ra mae me lo lo
Ah boo boo boo eee.
Boo boo eee boo eeee
La so lee lem
Lem lo lee da ung
Uhhh so ba boooo ohhhh.
Boo booo eee ung ba
Eee eee la looo
Lem lo lala la
Eeee oohhh ohhh ohhh ohhhh.

(He makes the soft, whispering sound imitating an explosion, and his entwined fingers come apart in a gesture that has the fingers and whatever they held going upward. **RICHIE** *and* **ROGER** *are near, as the lingering light fades to black.)*

Also by
David Rabe...

**The Basic Training of
Pavlo Hummel**

The Black Monk

The Dog Problem

Goose and Tomtom

Hurlyburly

In the Boom Boom Room

The Orphan

Sticks and Bones

Those the River Keeps

OTHER TITLES AVAILABLE FROM SAMUEL FRENCH

HURLYBURLY
David Rabe

Drama / 4m, 3f / Interior
This riveting drama took New York by storm in a production
directed by Mike Nichols and starring William Hurt, Sigourney
Weaver, Judith Ivey, Christopher Walken, Harvey Keitel, Cynthia
Nixon and Jerry Stiller. Characters nose deep in the decadent,
perverted, cocaine culture that is Hollywood, pursing a sex crazed,
drug-addled vision of the American Dream.

"...Offers some of Mr. Rabe's most inventive and disturbing
writing. At his impressive best, Mr. Rabe makes grim, ribald and
surprisingly compassionate comedy out of the lies and ationaliza-
tions that allow his alienated men to keep functioning if not feeling in the fogs of lotusland. They work in an industry so corrupt
that its only honest executives are those who openly admit that
they lie.

"Fresh, funny...a memorable play, imbued with a somehow com-
forting philosophy: that the messes and disappointments of life
are as much a part of its beauty as romantic love and chocolate
ice cream, and a perfect punch line can be as sublime as the
most wrenchingly lovely aria.""
– *The New York Times*

"An important work, masterfully accomplished."
– *Time*

"A powerful permanent contribution to American drama...Rivet-
ing, disturbing, fearsomely funny...Has a savage sincerity and a
crackling theatrical vitality. This deeply felt play deserves as wide
an audience as possible."
– *Newsweek*

OTHER TITLES AVAILABLE FROM SAMUEL FRENCH

STICKS AND BONES
David Rabe

Drama / 5m, 2f / Interior

A devastating portrait of a foolish, intolerant middle class American family. When the oldest son returns from Vietnam blinded the mother, a religious hypocrite and racial bigot invades his privacy and is too self-centered to be concerned with his plight. The father is a hypocrite and a failure. He has a double standard as to relations with women. The younger son is not only stupid, but a sexist pig as well. Then there's a sadistic, garrulous American Catholic priest who's programmed by textbooks. The family conspire to help the blind son to commit suicide. It's to be done in a very tidy, decent way. And in the finale, there's a searing, surrealistic scene in which bodies of the war's victims are seen.

Special Award of the New York Critics' Circle

"Strikingly original anti-war play...POWERFUL."
– *New York Daily News*

"A funny, cruel, mordant, unsparing attack on American society."
– WCBS TV